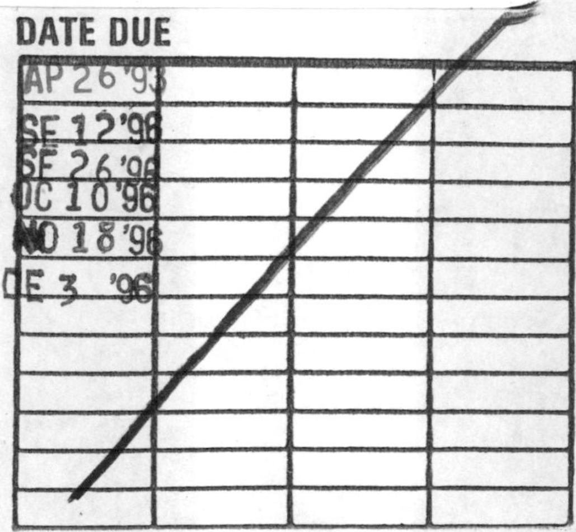
DATE DUE
AP 26 '93
SE 12 '96
SE 26 '96
OC 10 '96
NO 18 '96
DE 3 '96

BILLIE SOL

BILLIE SOL

KING OF TEXAS WHEELER-DEALERS

by Pam Estes

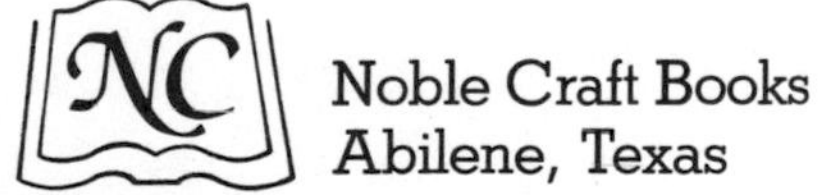

Noble Craft Books
Abilene, Texas

Library of Congress Catalog Card No. 83-51354

ISBN 0-915733-00-5

First Edition

Printed in the United States of America

ACKNOWLEDGEMENTS

I wish to thank the people who helped make this book a reality—my Daddy and Mother for sharing their knowledge with me; my brother and sisters for allowing me to tell others about our lives; my Uncle, John L. Estes, for assisting me with information concerning Daddy's early life; my grandmother, Lillian Estes, for sharing her pictures; my ex-husband, Walter Tedford, for encouraging me to work on the book during the 13 years of our marriage; my daughters, Tricia and Amy Joy, for their patience and cooperation in letting me work on this; my typists, Pam Jay and Teri Gauld; my secretary, Mary Parrish for her typing and making my office run smoothly while I worked on the book; to Paul Clolery for copy editing.

I am especially grateful to John Matthews for helping rewrite the manuscript; my editor, James Lenamon for his suggestions; and my publisher, Noble A. Craft for believing enough in the story to put it in print.

You win by losing,
Hold on by letting go,
increase by diminishing, and
Multiply by dividing.

—Billie Sol Estes

DEDICATION

This book is dedicated to my mother and father, my brother and sisters, my uncles, aunts, cousins, and grandparents. . . and all wheeler-dealers.

FOREWORD

When Pam asked me to write a foreword for her book, my first thought was that I didn't want to discuss the past, and regretted the book being written. I would rather forget the past. If I could relive the past, like most everyone, I would change many things. I never allowed myself the luxury of thinking about how things could have been.

I hadn't taken Pam's book very seriously, but when she said to me, "Daddy, I've sold the book. I've gotten my first advance check." Well, I knew it was serious business if some publisher had put down actual cash for Pam's book. So, I asked her to let me see the manuscript when it was finished. As I read her manuscript, I began looking back over the past 20 years in a way I had never before done. I was then glad that my story would be preserved for my grandchildren and for history.

I have not tried to influence what Pam wrote about me. But, I have spent many hours talking with her about all the events in my life that have brought me here to Big Spring Prison Camp. She has examined court records and newspapers and has talked to numerous people who were involved with me during the last 20 years. She has made up her own mind about the events that landed me in and out of prisons for 20 years. I believe this book is a fair representation of events as they occurred.

"In talking with people about you," Pam said to me, "the thing that interests them most is not how you got sent to prison, but how you got rich in the first place. If you will tell me your secrets of how you became a multimillionaire so young, I would like to share them with the people who read my book," she said.

I thought about how to make money and, to me, that is one of the easiest things in life to do. These are my 12 steps on how to get rich:

1. Get up early. Plan your day positively. Do something good for each person you see. A sense of humor is essential.
2. Have faith in yourself and your business deal. Get a deal that will work and make money, and then others will join you. You won't have to find people—they will find you.
3. Get good legal and accounting advice.
4. Hire the best people available. They will make you money. Delegate to others what they do better than you.
5. Have zeal and enthusiasm. Start a fire within you. Some will come join you, others just to watch you burn.
6. Be original and mysterious. Don't try to be like everyone else; hold back a part of yourself. Don't tell all of your innermost thoughts and feelings.
7. Share yourself. Love your fellow man. Cast your bread upon the wates. You will multiply by dividing.
8. Be competitive. That's the American way. Get in the last lick. He who laughs last does laugh best.
9. Live life to the fullest, a day at a time, and make each day your best.
10. Take risks and borrow to the limit to back your

ventures. The best fruit is at the end of the limb.

11. Learn from your failures. Forgive the past and at all costs, keep moving.
12. Be willing to listen. Be ready, and when the big play arrives, recognize it and go for it with all you've got.

Spending the prime of your life in prison takes the bloom off early riches. I can't say that money has been very important to me the last 20 years. It wouldn't sustain me here in prison, even if the government had let me keep it.

Your real wealth is your family, friends, God and Country. There is no way I know of that money could replace the sustenance and strength my family has given me during the years I have been in prison.

I, like Solomon, accumulated and accomplished all I dreamed of; but, in the end, it was all worthless. It took my crash to help me realize the real values of life. I would be a poor man if all I had waiting for me when I get out of prison was a pile of money. Fortunately, my family has stood by me. They are all the riches I have or need.

Billie Sol Estes
Big Spring, Texas

CONTENTS

BILLIE SOL

INTRODUCTION

Déjà Vu

Today I had a dream. I dreamed we were all safe and happy, and Daddy was still the richest man in West Texas. I dreamed I was a child again back in our Pecos mansion, where friends were gathered on the patio and steaks were barbecuing on the grill. Servants were bustling and children were splashing in the pool. Mother was relaxed and smiling, and Daddy was holding me in his lap.

But, when I awoke, I realized it was only a dream.

I was lying on a cold marble floor in a public restroom at the Federal Courthouse in Dallas. The jury had just come in with a guilty verdict and Daddy would be going back to prison. We weren't rich. We were broke. We weren't happy and safe. We were broken-hearted and harassed. I pulled myself up out of my fainting fit and returned to the courtroom.

I had been through all this before in 1962. Now it was 1979.

Daddy sat in a chair at the defense table. He had just been convicted of conspiracy to conceal assets even though the prosecution admitted they could find no evidence of assets to conceal.

The conviction would be allowed to stand even though one of the jurors later swore that he voted, under duress, against his true convictions. "Not sufficient for a mistrial," said the judge.

What the court was able to prove beyond a shadow of a doubt was that my Daddy is Billie Sol Estes. All they had to do to convince people that he was a crook was to say his name. His name has become a synonym for "big swindle." His first conviction 20 years ago helped make the career of Bobby Kennedy. Daddy's silence also allowed Lyndon Johnson to become President. Kennedy employed 76 FBI agents full time in addition to a support staff at an enormous cost to make sure that Lyndon Johnson's friend, Billie Sol, would be found guilty.

Daddy's second conviction in Dallas 15 years later, similarly made the prosecutor because he was able to show beyond the shadow of a doubt that the name "Billie Sol Estes" is synonymous with "swindle." To do so, the United States government employed full-time undercover agents, wired for sound, who wormed their way into our lives and recorded every word we said to each other and to our friends. They tapped our telephones and harassed our friends. They dragged ten hours of tapes of our private and intimate conversations into court and exposed us to mockery and ridicule.

Twenty years ago, the judge and prosecutor brought TV cameras into the courtroom of Daddy's trial because they were anxious to make their careers. The fact the conviction was overturned because of its circus-like atmosphere was the last bit of justice Daddy received in our judicial system. I often wonder if we could get that conviction overturned if it were to happen today. It frightens me to think that we probably could not.

MY DADDY WAS A MILLIONAIRE before he was 30; named one of the "Outstanding Young Men of Texas;" one of the Jaycees' "Outstanding Young Men of the United States," and was a friend of Lyndon Baines Johnson.

His rise to fame and riches came easily and quickly. His fall shook Wall Street and embarrassed Washington. He built an empire in the West Texas desert in the 50s, his land stretching farther than the eye could see. He owned oil wells, cotton and livestock. His elevators stored millions of bushels of grain, and he had a dozen other businesses throughout Texas.

He was a patriot who loved the American system and an optimist who believed in God. He thought if you trusted in Him, no wrong could befall you. He trusted everyone he met. He thought there was nothing he could not do.—And, for a little while, the life he led proved it to be true. While imprisoned, he often said, "I would rather be in jail in this country than free anywhere else in the world."

In 1961 he was appointed to John F. Kennedy's National Cotton Advisory Council. He had the potential to become a senator or governor of Texas. Daddy worshipped Lyndon Baines Johnson and the Democratic Party, making large campaign contributions to the party's candidates. Johnson, like Daddy, came from a Texas pioneer family. Autographed pictures of LBJ, John Kennedy, Sam Rayburn and close friend Ralph Yarborough hung on the walls of his office. Daddy was a familiar figure in Washington. He had a group of Texans flown to Washington for JFK's birthday and his inauguration anniversary party.

To help the campaign effort of Senator Ralph Yarborough, Daddy roasted two steers in our barbeque pit. Politicians seemed to like my bumbling but fascinating Texas millionaire father. He added color to their gatherings. His attorney once said he resembled an unmade bed. He was a good "token Texan" when the occasion called for it, and he was a soft touch to fill tables at $100 a plate.

Now that Daddy has been disgraced, it wouldn't matter how much money he gave the Party, he couldn't get invited to a public rally. Where Daddy's name was once magic in political circles, it now has the same impact as the word "plague" in a hospital waiting room or "fire" in a crowded theater.

Daddy, in his pyramiding rise to the top, made lots of friends and enemies—good friends and strong enemies. Most people who met Daddy either loved or hated him.

At the close of the 50s, his enemies were quietly gathering forces. The pyramid he built seemed solid. His cotton was tall, his grain elevators were full, and the land under the cotton held hidden reservoirs of oil. Our family was flourishing, and we lived in a palace in an oasis, with servants who had worked for Hollywood stars. We had a chauffeured limousine and flew in our own planes. Daddy loved everyone and everything and was on top of his world. He had it made like the Vanderbilts, the Murchisons, the Hunts. He was one of Texas' "fair-haired boys"—all of his deams had come true. It seemed he could do no wrong and was universally loved for his Midas touch.

Suddenly, Daddy was sitting in Pecos Jail. The government had seized his planes, and Robert Kennedy had sent investigators to our small town in the desert. Daddy had been indicted on numerous counts of numerous charges—fraud, mail fraud, and anti-trust violations, to name a few.

His bail was $500,000, the largest ever set in Texas at that time. When Daddy's brother, Uncle John L., called for help from "Billie's friends," LBJ was unavailable, and Yarborough, whom Daddy had helped seat in the Senate, said, "Billie Sol Who?" The government froze his assets, threw him into bankruptcy, and took his cotton, oil and grain. Our butler, chauffeur, cook and maids left. Mother, my brother, my sisters and I were in a state of shock. Daddy's friends were mostly in hiding.

He became one of the most infamous men in the country. His name surfaced everywhere from TV quiz shows to economics and history books. He was no longer Texas' "fair-haired boy." His name was seldom printed again without added tags as "bankrupt financier," "notorious swindler" or "former Texas boy wonder." What happened to Billie Sol Estes, the young man who was on top of the world—and could do no wrong?

Daddy was close to many elected government officials. He knew how they got and kept power. He told me recently, "I had the opportunity to influence who would be President, Vice President, Senator, Governor. When I was indicted, I could have involved many politicians, but I decided that when I went to prison, I would go alone.

He has kept his silence until now.

I CHAPTER

The Origin of the Wheeler-Dealer

Daddy's great grandfather, William Newton Estes, was born August 8, 1831, at Fort Payne, Alabama. He died at age 32, in the 1868 Battle of Chicamanugha, leaving behind his wife, Christie Ann McCampbell, five sons and two daughters. Shortly before his death he had been promoted to Colonel in the Confederate Army.

After the war, his widow decided to move her family westward to Texas, hoping to find more opportunity. Her relatives tried to discourage her from going west, warning, "You could run into Indians." She replied, "I hope I do. I'm part Indian myself."

It was a warm summer day in 1868 when her covered wagon stopped in Clyde, Texas, under the shade of a clump of oak trees near where the Clyde Church of Christ now stands. According to my grandfather, "She was a Methodist, having been baptized for the remission of sins, and she was taking communion." Her five sons and two daughters soon found work on nearby ranches, the girls working as cooks, and the boys working with cattle.

It was Solomon Burns, her fourth son, who became my great granddaddy. He made his living trading land and ranching in the Clyde area. He married Allie Vandelia Hancock on January 8, 1859, in Baird, Texas. Their sixth son, John Levi Estes, is my grandfather. He was born September 20, 1900, near Clyde, and was one of seven children. My daddy was named after John Levi's younger brother, Dr. Sol B. Estes, a well-loved and respected Abilene physician who died in 1982.

As a young man, John Levi, or "Papa John" as we grandchildren called him, attended Abilene Christian College to study to become a preacher.

He first saw Lillian Coffman, my daddy's mother, through the window of a barn where a dance was in progress. Lillian, my "MaMa" later told her grandchildren, "I was a little bit popular and real good at dancing. John didn't dance at all since he belonged to the Church of Christ."

John and Lillian's first son, John Levi, Jr., was born a few miles west of Clyde, at Elmdale, in the home of my grandfather's youngest brother, Dr. Sol B. Estes. The baby was delivered by Dr. Jack Estes, one of my grandfather's cousins and the first of many Estes doctors.

Less than a year after the birth of their first son, John and Lillian moved to the Texas Panhandle near a small town named Allen Reed, where my father was born. Papa John could have bought as much land there as he wanted for $3.00 an acre, but MaMa wanted to move back near Abilene so the children could attend Abilene Christian College. Later they returned to the Abilene area, to a small community named Hamby, where they bought 320 acres from their uncle, John Morrisett, for $67 per acre.

While living at Allen Reed, and just 18 months after John L., Jr. was born, Daddy was born. During the worst blizzard of the year, Papa John rode his horse to their nearest neighbors, the Words, to telephone for a doctor. MaMa's labor lasted all day and most of the night. By the time Daddy was born, snow was piled high on all sides of the house.

My grandmother recalls the doctor estimated Daddy's weight at just three pounds. The doctor called him Blizzard Bill, so MaMa and Papa John decided to name him "Billie." He was named "Sol" after Dr. Solomon Estes.

Papa John had raised the cash for Daddy's delivery by selling some of his blue-ribbon, prize-winning hound dogs. Daddy later said there is no where to go but up when you are traded for hound dogs when you are born.

Daddy's sister, Joan (pronounced Jo-Ann), was also born at Allen Reed. Shortly after she was born the family moved back to Callahan County.

My Grandmother says Daddy was a "real sweet, pleasant baby." She says he was unusually smart at an early age. He had a keen memory. After she read a book to him once, he could recite it for the other children by looking at the pictures.

When Daddy started the first grade in Fairview, near Hamby, it was soon apparent that he had an appetite for mathematics, much like his father. MaMa says he "brought home lots of prizes for math." One of the major influences on Daddy as he grew up was Mrs. Thelma Berry, wife of John Berry, a Clyde rancher. Mrs. Berry taught grammar school at the two-room school house in Fairview. She was fond of Daddy and occasionally let him go with her husband to sell wool, rather than attend class, because she thought it was more practical and would help him more.

Mrs. Berry recalls that he had an unusual ability to do arithmetic and never needed to figure his math problems on paper. He did not concentrate as well in English, and his grammar is still poor. My Aunt Joan did all his reports for him.

When Daddy and Mother married in 1946, they married under a tree in front of the Berry's ranch house. And when Daddy was honored as one of the Ten Outstanding Young Men of the United States, Mrs. Berry went with them to Washington.

CHRISTMAS WAS THE BIGGEST EVENT of the year for Papa John's family. Their home was a center of activity for cousins, aunts and uncles.

MaMa and Papa John asked their children to write their letters to Santa Claus. The only request on Daddy's list when he was seven was for a "lamb, please." On Christmas Eve, MaMa loaded up her four children in her Model A to go to Clyde "to see the Christmas sights," which consisted mostly of displays in store fronts on Clyde's Main street. When they got back home about sunset, Santa Claus had already stopped by the Estes house. The Christmas tree was decorated, and each child had a gift. Daddy quickly spotted his gift, a woolly, little lamb tied to the tree. Mama said, "Billie Sol, this is Merry."

John Berry, husband of Daddy's beloved teacher, had a herd of sheep, and every year Merry, bred to one of Berry's rams, presented Billie with two lambs. Also, when John Berry lost a mother sheep, he would give Daddy the orphan lambs. He also let Daddy collect "dead wool," the wool from sheep that died in the pastures. Then Daddy would miss school to go with Mr. Berry to sell his wool.

Daddy saved $5.00 to buy another lamb by working at the Earl Hayes dairy for 50 cents a day. He had to be up at 3 o'clock every morning. This started a lifetime habit of rising before dawn and working while others were sleeping.

Papa John recalls that when Daddy was about eight or nine years old, Billie Sol wanted to have a man-to-man talk with his dad. He asked: "Just what is my part of the work around the farm?" Papa John said he would hire one of the other kids to do Billie Sol's part of the work so "he could be out trading." I think one reason for Daddy's success was his ability to delegate. He once saw me struggling with a problem in my own business and said, "Pam, you'll never make it in business if you don't learn to delegate. You are only one person. Let someone help you."

At age nine, Daddy's job was riding pasture with his mother. MaMa says, "We rode pasture in our Model A Ford. Billie Sol would ride on the hood and when we found a stray calf, Billie would jump off the hood and rope him. I would stop the car and worm the calf with some medicine."

Another time, Daddy sold a cow to a neighboring farmer, promising it would produce four gallons of milk. When it didn't, the farmer complained bitterly. Unabashed, Billie Sol said he had not guaranteed how long it would take the cow to deliver the four gallons.

From about the age 12, old Grandmother Estes (Papa John's mother, Vandelia) allowed Daddy to write checks on her bank account. MaMa says he was the only one of the kids allowed to do that because Grandmother Estes knew he could "tell a good deal when he saw it." One day he came home and said, "Mother, I bought a pig in Baird today. Will you go get him? I wrote a check on Grandmother's account."

She got in her Model A and drove six miles to Baird, picked up the hog and brought him back to the homeplace. Billie then "dressed him out," made sausage and sold it. He then paid back old Grandmother Estes, and he never failed to take her flowers and candy as interest on the loan.

Papa John recalls the time Daddy bought a neighbor's hog. Daddy saw the hog, estimated its weight and made the man an offer. Daddy gave him one of Grandmother Estes' checks. When the man found out the hog weighed in at more than his own estimate, he went to Papa John very angry. He insisted he had been cheated, and he wanted his money back. Papa John said, "You made a bargain, and you stick by it. Billie Sol just out-traded you."

DADDY'S FONDNESS FOR FRANKLIN D. Roosevelt and the Democratic Party began at an early age. When he was 15 years old, he wrote Roosevelt to ask if there was a government program to give relief for Callahan County. There had been a drought and everyone needed grain and water for their livestock. Daddy had been taught in school that the government was your friend and would give help when it was needed. President Roosevelt wrote back telling him about the surplus grain program. Daddy then went to his banking advisor, Bob Norrel of Baird, and got a commitment to borrow the money to buy the grain. He sent an order for 17 train cars of grain. The government wanted a down payment of $3,500. Daddy was a minor, but Norrel still loaned him the money.

An official from the U.S. Department of Agriculture was sent to Clyde. He went to the Estes' farm and asked to see Mr. Estes. Papa John said, "Oh, you mean my son. He's in school." The USDA official said, "Is he a teacher?" Papa John said, "No, he's a student." The USDA official said he couldn't give carloads of wheat to a high school kid, but later in the day when Daddy handed him the check for $3,500, he was satisfied.

The train was pulled onto a side track in Abilene at the T&P Railroad yard. Papa John wondered, "How's that crazy kid going to get the stuff unloaded in Abilene?" Daddy was thinking as he milked cows at 3 a.m., "I'll be hung if I am going to be milking cows at 3 a.m. for the rest of my life. There has got to be an easier way." He finished his milking, walked three miles to school, thinking all the way about how he would unload the grain, sell it, and get rich.

By the time school was out that afternoon, Daddy had a trailer hitched onto the back of his little red convertible. He filled the car with football players to help unload his wheat. He had already printed handbills advertising the wheat, and farmers had come with sacks to buy it. Daddy sold more than three million pounds of feed to Texas farmers.

Daddy had saved his customers about $50,000 compared to the local selling price. He repaid the loan to the bank and made a profit for himself. In 1968 when we began fighting to get Daddy out on parole, Norell the Baird banker, wrote to Lyndon Johnson:

Dear Mr. President:

Mr. Billie Sol Estes was reared in this county a few miles northwest of Baird. When he was a minor he did business with this bank with his father acting as surety, then when he reached the proper age he did business under his own name.

All our transactions were satisfactory and carried out to the letter.

The Estes family are pioneers in this section and are well known for their stability. We have always thought that certain events caused Billie Sol to be highly ambitious, but now we think that this experience has had a sobering effect upon him and he will drop back into a normal life with the sole ambition to make a good solid citizen, which we think he can do.

Yours very truly,

Robert (Bob) Norrel, President
The First National Bank of Baird
Baird, Texas

By the time Daddy was 15 years old, his flock had grown to more than 100 sheep. When he was 19, he owned about 60 Hereford cows, 50 steers and some hogs. He sold the wool and most of his sheep and cows for $3,000 and bought 400 sows and feeder pigs. Daddy estimated that by age 18, he had made about $38,000 from Merry, his first lamb.

During the Depression, MaMa churned butter and traded it for other food and supplies. Daddy's family was respected as hard-working people with a strong religious bent. The Estes were faithful members of the Church of Christ, and the Coffmans had been among the early founders of the Methodist Church in West Texas. John Estes was a lay preacher and Lillian taught a pre-school Bible class.

Papa John and MaMa are optimists. They instilled in their children the philosophy that all men are equal and can do anything with the help of God. They taught their children that regardless of what bad or good times might come, they should love and respect God, their family and their country.

On April 25, 1944, Daddy received the honor of speaking at the launching of the *SS O.B. Martin* at the Houston shipyard. The ship was named for O.B. Martin of Carroll, Texas, the famed father of Texas agriculture and former director of Texas A&M College Extension Service.

Daddy also represented more than 100,000 4-H Club members at the launching of the 10,500-ton Liberty Ship. Some 150 students from 15 counties within 150 miles of Houston attended the launching. Daddy received this honor because he was the National Blue Ribbon Achievement Champion, chosen in 1943 at the International Livestock Exposition in Chicago, Ill., where he met President Roosevelt. According to an article in the April 30, 1944, *Houston Chronicle* "Young Estes frequently borrows up to $5,000 at any of the banks in Callahan County near his cooperative feed store in Clyde, even though his signature, as a minor, would not be accepted where he is less well known."

DADDY'S OLDER BROTHER, JOHN L., was a serious boy. His goal in life was to be a doctor. He had a keen sense of responsibility for his younger brothers and sisters. John L. went into the Air Force after graduating from high school, and then to Abilene Christian College, where he received a Bachelor of Science degree. It was at ACC that John L. met and married June Linn.

After graduation from college, John L. taught school then attended dental school at the University of Texas Medical Branch, Houston. MaMa and Papa John had helped send him through Abilene Christian College while they still had children at home, so Daddy sent him through dental school. Uncle John L. later repaid Daddy by assisting my sisters, my brother and me through college and helping us while Daddy was in prison. For the first eight years Daddy was in prison, Uncle John L. was like a father to me. When I had problems, I turned to him and he was always there. When I married in 1969, he walked down the aisle with me, gave me away and paid for the wedding.

John L. didn't know, of course, that the money he was to earn as a dentist would one day be needed to support his brother's family and that he would have an opportunity to repay Daddy for his education. He proved that he was his brother's keeper. Uncle John L. was both criticized and praised for supporting his brother. He has a plaque over his desk in his office that says, "He's not heavy, he's my brother."

Bobby Frank Estes was the third son born to Papa John and MaMa. He was less outgoing and quieter than his two older brothers. Bobby and Daddy first worked together at an early age. When they were 10 and 12, they earned money by helping ranchers in Clyde clear their land of prickly pears. The government was paying ranchers to clear their land, and so the ranchers hired boys to do the work. Also, they raised cows and sheep which their parents had given them or which they bought with their earnings from doing chores. Daddy had always been the leader; Bob, the faithful follower.

In 1966, Bob had an operation. Although he returned home from the hospital, he was in pain for six months before he was hospitalized again. The doctors knew he had very little time to live, and they notified our family. Prison officials gave Daddy the choice of seeing him once before he died, or attending the funeral. Daddy wanted to see him once more, and so Uncle John L. had Daddy flown from Leavenworth. A guard accompanied him, and Daddy was allowed to stay a few hours.

Bob had been only semi-unconscious for several days. He was only taking water, a teaspoon at a time, for nourishment, and was speaking deliriously in Spanish, the language he had spoken to Mexicans on his farms in Pecos. When Daddy walked into the room, Bob turned to him and said, "Hi, Billie," just as though they had not been separated for several years. They had always been so close, never living more than a few blocks from each other until Daddy went away to prison. The last thing Bob said to Daddy was, "We'll be together again soon, Billie." Bob died a few days later and was buried in the family cemetery in Clyde.

Daddy has two sisters, both nurses. Joan married Alfred Lastovica, a jeweler in Temple, Texas. The youngest sister, Jean, lives in Clyde and is married to Kenneth Holcombe.

Daddy's youngest brother is Word Estes. Since he was born about 15 years after Daddy, he grew up with no brothers or sisters around. After graduating from high school, he came to live with us in Pecos until he married. He was handsome and just old enough to command our constant admiration. In 1961, he announced that he was marrying Juanita Baum, Daddy's secretary. Daddy said, "She was one of the smartest secretaries I ever had, and my kid brother stole her." Word wanted their four children to live in Clyde on the family farm, and he is in partnership with his dad in the real estate business.

He said recently, "If Billie gets in trouble again, 'they' are not going to get their hands on him again. We will just take him out to the north pasture and shoot him ourselves."

II CHAPTER

"The Best Deal I Ever Made"

Daddy was not very interested in girls before he reached high school. His mother says he was just too busy working and making money to worry about girls.

But he came home from school one day and said, "Mother, I met a girl today with the prettiest legs you have ever seen." Mama says he then became embarrassed for what he said. Mother was a quiet, shy girl. She was pretty and intelligent. She and Daddy began courting and neither one ever dated anyone else. Five years later, they were married. Mother had moved to Clyde in the middle of her sophomore year. Mother says she was "used to being the new girl in school" because she moved almost every year.

Daddy liked Mother from the moment he saw her. He smiles and says, "I always knew a good deal when I saw one, and she was the best deal I ever made."

Mother first remembers seeing Daddy across the school yard. She said "Mr. Bravery" was trying to get his friends to ask her to go on a date with him. Mother says: "He finally talked someone into asking me (he was always good at getting people to do things for him), and from then on we were courting steady."

Mother says Daddy was not like any of the other boys in school. He was 15 years old, and looked like he was at least 20. He had earned his own living expenses since he was seven years old. "He usually had more pocket money than most families had at home in their sugar bowls," she said. "He was always working and making money. But even though he always had money, he was never greedy and would share whatever he had."

Each morning he would wait in the school yard and give money to any student who couldn't buy his own lunch. Once a month, the entire school would get out early to attend a movie in Clyde. Daddy usually paid for most of the tickets. He was always sensitive to other peoples' lack of money. He knew he had the talent for making money, and one reason he loved making it was the extreme pleasure and pride he had in giving it away.

WHEN WORLD WAR II BEGAN, young men from Callahan County began leaving for war. Uncle John L. joined the Air Force and became a pilot. He flew B-17s. MaMa loves to tell about the day she was hanging clothes on the line to dry when a plane swooped down low. A few days later she got a letter from Uncle John L. saying it was his plane.

While Daddy's friends, brothers and cousins were in the service, Daddy was home in Clyde. As a child, he had a bone disease, Legg-Perthes. The disease caused Daddy to have a short leg and pains in his back, so he was unable to serve. Though he was unable to fight, he did perform an important service. It was estimated that in 1942, he fed out and sold 44 calves and fed the equivalent of 111 fighting men. MaMa said a friend sent her a newspaper clipping about her son serving his country, suggesting that Daddy should be off fighting, too.

In 1944, Daddy joined the Maritime Service. It was the only branch that would accept him because of his bad leg. At age 20, when he joined the service, he had 60 white-faced cows, 50 steers, a pasture full of hogs and money in the bank. In 1981 when Daddy was in prison and needed hospitalization, the government couldn't find his military records. He quipped, "I guess they took my V.A. benefits, too."

LIKE ANY SERVICE MAN MANY miles away from home, Daddy wrote Mother a letter almost every day while he was away. The following is a typical example. Note the last paragraph, which now it seems very prophetic:

Letters
6

Janaury 15, 1945

Dearest Darling,

Hon, how is my darlin'g.

Hon, I got off to go to church one hour this morning. Hon it's pretty cold up here. It's 0° weather. We fell out at five this morning. Just got in. It's now nine o'clock. Hon, we've went and all day we have been moving snow off the silly watches, gosh it's cold. Hon, I like my work fine. I think we will have to fall out about 2 o'clock in the morning. We worked until 12:20 last night shoveling snow. Hon, lots of guys are dropping out into the army after boot camp. Hon, I will start all over again because I dread to fail, hon. Hon, when I get home I am going to be the happiest boy in the world and the sweetest. Darling, I am on the run all the time. I feel fine though. Hon I will write you some more when I get rested. Hon, write me lots. Hon, I really do like it fine.

Hon, a bunch of boys who left from here on a Wednesday night went to sea on a ship. It blew up, killed nearly all of them. They were just fine neighbors. Hon, I am laying in my bunk, where one of them slept.

One of the boys who was killed was sleeping in the same bunk I am. I got his when he left. You probably read it in the paper.

Honey, how's every thing at home. I hope you are O.K.

Letters
7

> *Hon, write me lots. Just know I don't know what I am going to do. Hon, I will want to tell you about it when I get rested more.*
>
> *Hon, I have been thinking lots darling. Hon, when I get home I want to be with you and be happy. Hon I have always worshipped money. That's where my greatest failing has been. Hon, I really miss you more than I could ever tell you.*
>
> *Honey, be sweet, I will close,*
> *Goodnight darling,*
> *All my love*
> *Sol*

MOTHER AND DADDY WERE MARRIED July 14, 1946, on the ranch lawn of John Berry. "We had always visited John and Mrs. Berry, Sol's favorite teacher, so we wanted to be married there," Mother says. "Sol never liked to go to picture shows for entertainment, he just liked making money or talking about making money. We were just going to get married at home, so Mrs. Berry wanted us to get married at her ranch."

They had planned a honeymoon trip to Ruidoso, N. M. "We made it as far as the Windsor Hotel in Abilene, and we spent our first married night there," Mother said. "The next day we went to Sweetwater, just 40 miles from Abilene, and stayed at the Bluebonnet, but then we went back to Clyde to set up housekeeping. Sol said we could honeymoon later. Of course we never did. He was always 'closing a big deal.' We lived with Grandmother Coffman for several months, then we rented another old house in the country. When Pamela was about to be born, we moved into Clyde. She was born premature after I had rearranged the furniture. Sol came in on the tractor."

DADDY WAS GETTING CONTRACTS FOR clearing prickly pear cactus and was moving barracks that he bought from the government. Government regulation said that barracks could not be sold as individual housing in the same town. To be sold, they had to be moved from town to town. For instance, barracks bought in Bastrop had to be moved to Austin, and barracks in Austin had to be switched to Bastrop.

In one of Daddy's many letters to me from prison, he wrote, "I bought up the barracks in Texas, Arkansas, California and New Mexico." MaMa says they would send Uncle Bob to make the bids because he was "sort of careless looking. He would blend into the crowd like a chameleon. Billie Sol was too noticeable."

After they bought the barracks, the whole family got into the act of selling them. They flew in a single-engine plane to inspect them, and MaMa would decide how they should be cut up to have the best floor plan. She would draw a blueprint for each individual house.

Papa John would oversee the moving and selling. MaMa says when she drives to Arizona she can still see the small houses along the highway.

Grandmother says they tried to send Daddy to college. "He had scholarships," MaMa said, "but he just didn't have the time. He just wanted to make money, but he made sure his brother Johnny went."

Papa John says Daddy "just wasn't satisfied with being a country farmer. He wanted to get bigger and bigger." He said from the time Daddy was a little boy, he always did what he wanted to do. He said: "It's those dern, crooked politicians that got my boy in trouble."

III CHAPTER

Daddy's Poor Little Rich Girl

Whenever we traveled, it was by plane or limousine. Our plane seated seven people fairly comfortably. Daddy had gotten his first plane back in the early 50s when he was buying and selling army barracks. From that time on we always had at least one plane, and frequently two, available for family use. Our pilot was Doug Lusader. His wife smoked cigarettes, which made her very rare in our circle of friends. Once when she was in our home, she burned a hole in the dining room table, and to this day when I see that place on the table, I always think of her. Doug was a very good pilot and never caused us any worry.

When boarding the plane, we would have to seat ourselves so that we achieved the best weight distribution. Daddy had to ride in the front of the plane because he was so heavy, and because I was always overweight, I had to sit right behind the pilot. Then my brother and sisters would squeeze onto the little bench seat. The plane was always hot and uncomfortable until we got up into the air. We would then take bets on who was going to vomit, because invariably, someone did.

We took along lots of snacks on these flights; peanuts, popcorn, soft drinks and magazines to read. By the time we would reach our destination, the plane would need to be cleaned because of the mess. After leaving the plane, someone would come and clean it so it would be ready for our return.

I remember those plane trips as always being a pleasure, but there were a few hairy moments. One of the most memorable trips occurred when I was 11 or 12. We were flying high up in the clouds and I was polishing my fingernails on the little pull-down tray table, when all of a sudden a window blew open. The plane immediately started dropping and we nearly all got killed, but because of our confidence in Doug, we didn't even get frightened.

Daddy always slept from the minute we got into a car or plane. No matter where we went or how long we traveled, he slept. When traveling by car, Mother had to drive because he was such a poor driver.

I remember one trip from Pecos to Clyde in our limousine. All five children were in the back and the two maids were on the jump seats. When we arrived in Abilene, we pulled into Casey's Drive-in Restaurant on South First Street. It was the local hangout at that time. I remember how embarrassed we were when people in the other cars started pointing at us and laughing. Daddy waved at everyone—told us to be quiet and ordered nine hamburgers, nine fries, and nine Cokes. Daddy ordered the hamburgers with no variations, so when we got them we rudely rolled down the windows and I pitched out my tomatoes, Jan threw out her onions and Dawn threw out her pickles. It's easy to behave like spoiled brats when you are indulged as we were.

Sometimes, though, Daddy's indulgences were more irritating than pleasurable. More than once I came home to find that Daddy had given away all of my clothes. I mean *all* my underwear, shoes, everything. If he met someone who had a little girl my size who didn't have many clothes, he would give her mine. Then he would say, "Well, you just go and get whatever you need."

Our home would have been just another big house in Dallas or Houston or Beverly Hills, but in Pecos, Texas, it was a palace. When Daddy bought it in 1952, it was a flat-top house built over an old swimming pool. The basement always had a little water standing in it. Mother tried to keep us kids locked out of the basement, but we managed to get in despite being a little bit scared to go there. We believed there were rattlesnakes in the basement.

One of the strongest impressions I have of my childhood was that there was always an abundance of everything: money, love and food. Our basement held three freezers full of meat, fresh vegetables and fruits and shelves of canned goods.

The main part of the first house consisted of two bedrooms, two baths, a living room and a den. The next addition was Daddy's study and a guest bedroom. As the family expanded and Daddy's fortune grew, we added a second story. The upstairs became the special domain for my three sisters and myself. We each had our own bedroom. Mother let us select our own color scheme and carpet. It was a decorator's nightmare but a delight to us and to our many friends.

My first room was yellow with yellow carpet. Splatter paint was "in," so the color of my room was a putrid blend of several colors of paint applied with an air brush. I later decided I hated the gray and black specks on the yellow walls, so Daddy had it sanded. We then painted the room lilac—all the walls, closets, custom-built furniture and shelves. Then we installed plush lilac carpet.

I now had a lilac haven where I could listen to Pat Boone's "Anastasia," the Big Bopper and "Chantilly Lace," and Buddy Holly and "Teen Angel." I could climb out the upstairs window to go to a neighbor's house to see Elvis Presley on Ed Sullivan's TV show because Mother wouldn't let us watch it. I loved Elvis, but Mother thought he was "just plain sinful and disgusting." Years later in 1974, when we attended one of his concerts in Abilene, Mother got the binoculars and wouldn't turn them loose.

My sister Jan was born May 20, 1950. Her room was mint green with touches of pink. She loved to ride horses. Homer, our chauffeur, drove her to the stables each morning. Jan took all the dolls from her shelves and replaced them with baseball bats, gloves, horse bridles and tennis rackets.

The third Estes child was another girl. They named her Dawn, and she was born in Pecos on May 21, 1952. Her room was blue and white. We were all jealous because she had a canopy bed—and a monkey. When the monkey died of pneumonia, the news made the society page of a Pecos newspaper.

In December, 1954, Daddy announced the arrival of Billie Sol Estes, Jr. He was so happy to have a son he passed out cigars by the box. Billie's room was located next to Daddy's office. I don't remember it very well because Billie always stayed with us girls. He loved to sleep with me and called me the "marshmallow," white and soft, and said he "didn't need a pillow when he slept with Pam."

Our baby sister, Joy, was born on September 5, 1956 and was named Lillian Joy, after Daddy's mother. She had a room colored pink from its ceiling to the plush carpet. She was only 5-years old when we left Pecos, and she always clung to me. Her early memories are of the years we spent in courtrooms.

There were two wings extending from the main part of the house, making an "L" shape. One wing was a 55-foot living room which had a beautifully polished flagstone floor, Spanish furniture and glass walls. At the end of the room we had palm trees, other plants and Dawn's monkey, Cheeta, in his cage. We loved to entertain there.

The final addition to the house was the "Truman Wing," so named because Daddy's political hero, Harry S. Truman, was expected to visit. But he never did. There were several rooms downstairs in the basement. One large room had been fixed up for the maids' quarters. Maria and Julia, two sisters, lived there and had their own kitchen, living area and bedroom.

The grounds around the house were lush by desert standards. Daddy imported three large palm trees from Florida. The house was located on a city block and had between 6,000 and 7,000 square feet of floor space. We had a patio with a ramp for roller skating, a rose garden and a large, custom-built barbeque pit equipped with garden hoses. Daddy always barbequed with a water hose in one hand because he never had time to let the coals burn down properly and the flames had to be periodically tamed. The pit had the capacity to barbeque two steers at one time. We also had a little pink trailer house in the backyard which we used for a play house and which caught fire on more than one occasion from our cooking.

We also had two tennis courts because Jan liked tennis. We kept the nets rolled up most of the time so we could use the courts for a roller skating rink and a race track for Jan's gocart and Billie's little Model T with an engine.

Our swimming pool caused a lot of amused gossip in Pecos. Mother and Daddy, being members of the Church of Christ, did not believe in mixed bathing. We had an eight-foot fence around the pool to keep the neighbor's children from drowning and to prevent neighbors from looking in. Mother allowed only mixed (male and female) swimming with immediate family members and very small children. When we had large groups over for swimming parties, the women and girls swam for an hour, then the men and boys.

OUR CHRISTMASES WERE SPECTACULAR. Mother would decorate the house and most of our relatives would come and spend the holidays with us. On Christmas Eve, Daddy liked to dress in his Santa Claus suit, and, accompanied by his children, deliver toys and candy to underprivileged children in Pecos. One of his nicknames in Pecos was "Santa Sol." He was well-known for giving hams and turkeys to everyone he knew.

I often used to hear that rich people were miserable and never happy, but we were the exception to that rule. We loved our home and we entertained lavishly and frequently. However, no alcoholic beverages were ever served in our home because of our religious beliefs.

IN 1961, DADDY HAD A BIG POLITICAL rally and picnic for Senator Ralph Yarborough. Our regular household staff and some temporary help had been working for several weeks preparing for the party. Two steers were roasted in the barbecue house. Slim Willet's country and western band from Abilene provided entertainment. Their most famous song was "Don't Let the Stars Get in Your Eyes." It was one of Daddy's favorite songs.

Hundreds of people attended that picnic and Ralph Yarborough raised a great deal of money, most of it coming from Daddy—in cash. During that time, Daddy had been supplying Lyndon

Johnson with large infusions of cash, not only for his own political needs, but for people Johnson, himself, chose to help. Sometimes, Johnson would send people like Ralph Yarborough directly to Daddy for fund raising help. On other occasions, Johnson would get bundles of cash from Daddy and distribute it himself. Since these transactions were all cash, there is no reliable way of knowing how much money went to Johnson or what became of it. Daddy has steadfastly refused to talk about that part of his life with anyone, even me.

UNTIL ABOUT 1959, MOTHER DID ALL the cooking at our house and most of the housekeeping with the help of two maids, Maria and Julia Jasso, who lived with us. Then, in 1960, Daddy hired Homer and Wilma Hardin. Homer was our chauffeur and butler, and he did a little cooking. Wilma cooked and did some housekeeping. I don't believe Mother liked having them around the house. Homer and Wilma had worked in California for a number of celebrities, they said, including Merle Norman.

Homer and Wilma were the talk of Pecos. I still remember how embarrassed I was the first time Homer took me to Woolworth's. When I was ready to get out of the limousine, Daddy's pride and joy, Homer took off his cap, bowed from the waist and opened the door. In Pecos, Texas, people just didn't go to Woolworth's in a chauffeur-driven limousine. This was one of those things that caused Daddy to be ridiculed. In New York or Philadelphia in 1960, it might have been okay, but not in Pecos, Texas. One thing about Daddy that endears him to me but causes others to laugh, is that he isn't aware of ridicule or animosity and jealousy in others. He is not humiliated or embarrassed.

Homer did perform one useful function. Daddy needed a

chauffeur. Daddy was a terrible driver. He simply could not concentrate on the road. He got several tickets for going the wrong way down one-way streets, failing to stop at stop signs and speeding. He often had his driver's license suspended.

DADDY IS ALWAYS ON ONE EXTREME or another, either extravagant or pinching every penny. My sister says one of her most poignant memories is of Daddy on a money-saving spree. He put diesel fuel in the limousine and ruined the engine.

IV CHAPTER

Multiply by Dividing

Since he didn't have a large inheritance to give him a running start, many people are curious about how Daddy got so rich at such a young age. In an earlier chapter, I've told how Daddy parlayed a lamb into a $38,000 fortune in just a few years time—a sizeable sum in the Depression 30s for a young man.

At the risk of oversimplifying, it's safe to say that Daddy's first $100 million was just a continuation of that same process. Daddy always used whatever he had as leverage to get something else. It's a basic principle of business, the major difference being that Daddy's levers always had a longer pry bar than anyone else's. He could almost literally use a thimble to collateralize a diamond.

Daddy was also willing to take monumental risks, a factor that served him well until things started coming apart, and then risk-taking worked against him.

Perhaps the most significant factor in Daddy's spiral to success was his almost mystical ability to get other people to do things for him. He could get people to do things that would later cause them to say, "I don't know why I did that." This, more than anything else, got Daddy into trouble. Many people who sold Daddy their credit for a high interest rate later tried to claim that they were swindled. Despite the prosecution testimony to show that Daddy had conned people into helping collateralize his enterprises—all of them had acted willingly—and many of them would do it all over again.

THE WAY DADDY ACQUIRED THE FARM in Earth, Texas, is typical of the way he operates. He had always wanted an irrigated farm so he could "make a crop when it forgot to rain." He had gone to Earth in 1949, to arrange for his brother Bob to haul a load of wheat to market for a farmer, Dub Cook. Mr. Cook had recently suffered a heart attack, and the doctor told him that he had to move somewhere quiet to avoid another one. Daddy said, "I have a house in Clyde about like yours," so they simply traded.

It was while he was living in Earth that he began to form his dream of an irrigated farm empire around Pecos. He had been interested in that part of the state since he had stopped there on a trip to New Mexico in the late 40s. When he finally did move to Pecos, he was said to have arrived "with nothing more than a battered briefcase." But he also had land that was paid for, a good deal of cash and years of experience and an understanding of agriculture. Still, today, when my family reads a story that includes the "battered briefcase" phrase, we read no further because we recognize it as one of those untrue stories that are copied and recopied by reporters.

JAN AND I WERE BABIES WHEN WE moved to Pecos in the early 50s, and even though Daddy had cash to buy land, he didn't have any left over to buy us a house. So we shared an apartment with some people he had known back near Abilene, Ansel and Eula Hendricks and their two children. Ironically, the apartment was in an old Air Force barrack like the ones Daddy had sold all over the country. Mother says the apartment was in the worst part of town. It had one bedroom, and there were eight of us living there.

We lived there several months, then Mother and Daddy rented a small house in Pecos that Daddy later bought.

I was three at the time we moved to Pecos I was six when we moved into the house built over the swimming pool and by the time I was eight we had the nicest house in Pecos.

Mother was horrified when she drove into Pecos for the first time. It was very, very hot, there was no air conditioning, and dust was blowing. She almost put her foot down at that point and said she wasn't going to live there; but since Daddy had always been successful at whatever he did, and despite her misgivings, she was determined to trust him and decided to make the most of living there.

Daddy was the first person to irrigate in the Pecos area. Before he came, the land was largely unproductive desert and not worth much. He soon changed all that, and before he was through, the value of land in that part of the country had skyrocketed, making a lot of other people rich as well as Daddy. As a matter of fact, many people who later accused Daddy of fraud and who testified against him had seen the value of their land increase at least four-fold as a direct result of the farming revolution Daddy started.

Daddy became a millionaire within two years after he moved to Pecos. How did he get so rich in such a short time? What people want to know is his get-rich formula in the simplest terms. I think I can summarize the process in a few statements.

First, he bought lots of cheap land. He sold his other farms, which enabled him to buy three or four acres of Pecos land for each acre sold in Clyde or Earth.

Once he had the land, he doubled its productivity and its value by irrigation. Pecos farmers had tried irrigation before but the high cost of electricity for pumping the water had defeated them. Daddy located the nearest natural gas pipeline then spearheaded an effort to get it extended to the Pecos area so that irrigation pumps could be driven by less expensive natural gas. This in turn expanded his credit, which allowed him to purchase more land.

He introduced the use of anhydrous ammonia, and once again doubled the productivity and the value of the land.

He began to buy all the agriculture-related businesses in the Pecos area until he had a near monopoly. With the explosion of the agriculture economy, there was to be a rapid growth of such things as farm implements and supplies—including anhydrous ammonia and fertilizer tanks.

He knew how to use credit. Even though Daddy arrived in Pecos with enough cash to buy several hundred acres of land, that alone would not have been enough to produce as much as it would take to become truly rich. So, true to his policy, he always borrowed to the limits of his credit. At that point, and up to the point he was arrested, he had a spotless credit record that went back to the time he was a young boy.

If Daddy had stopped right there he probably would still be the richest man in West Texas, but he had a fatal flaw, and, ironically, it was a kind of innocent generosity that triggered the chain of events that was to bring him down and change our lives forever.

That generosity compelled Daddy to give large sums of money to the Democratic Party. The more he gave, the more he made—and the more his influence in Washington grew. The more he made, the more he needed—and so he took bigger and bigger risks. Daddy, who had grown up during the Depression, believed Franklin Roosevelt was the savior of the nation and that the Democratic Party was the continuing embodiment of FDR's spirit. So he began, innocently at first, to give large sums of money to the Party fund as well as to candidates. The eventual result of all this generosity was that the Democrats in government became, at first, grateful and then increasingly helpful to Daddy. The Department of Agriculture, contrary to testimony at Senate hearings, began to show him how to take advantage of loopholes in the grain storage and other programs. Flattering as it may seem, he just didn't have the savvy to figure all the ins and outs of the programs himself. The Democratic Party felt its back had been scratched and was simply responding in kind.

Daddy's get-rich scenario was simple enough, and workable enough, but agricultural riches during the days of the great give-away programs could be considerably enhanced with the co-operation of the Agriculture Department. The Cotton Allotment Program was a good example of this.

In the early sixties, cotton production was strictly controlled in order to reduce surplus crops. The Agriculture Department wanted no new land planted in cotton; but Daddy wanted *all* his planted in cotton. He had more than 3,000 acres of land at one time but about half had never been planted in cotton and therefore didn't qualify for an allotment.

The regulations of the program allowed allotments to be transferred from one parcel of land to another in certain circum-stances. The regulation was designed to protect farmers whose cotton producing acreage had been taken out of production by state condemnation of the land for such things as widening roads, enlarging lakes or other public works projects. The regulation said that farmers who lost land this way could transfer their cotton allotments to other parcels of land, anywhere cotton could be grown. The farmers didn't have to personally farm the land, but they did have to actually own it to get the allotment transferred. However, whenever they sold the land, the allotment remained with the land.

Well, it didn't take Daddy long to figure out how to take advantage of that regulation. Daddy wanted those allotments so he could grow cotton on *all* his land in Pecos. He couldn't just buy the allotments. That would be illegal. So he, with the help of the Agriculture Department, figured out a way to get the allotments legally transferred to his land in Pecos. He would sell parcels of land to farmers who had allotments but no land, get the allotments transferred, then he would lease back the land from the farmers. The contract for the land sale stipulated that if the farmer defaulted on the first payment, the land title would revert to Daddy.

To make sure that the farmer would not want to retain possession of the land he had bought, each parcel was laid out in long narrow strips, sometimes as narrow as forty feet wide so that it never occupied an entire field. Such awkwardly shaped land parcels would be useless to anyone except Daddy. There was never any danger that the "purchaser" of the land would not default on the first payment. It was clearly understood that the first year's lease payment of $50 per acre was the purchase price of the allotment. This was a good deal for Daddy because farmland at that time without cotton allotments was selling for about $150 per acre, whereas land with cotton allotments was fetching about $300 per acre. It was a good deal for the farmer selling the allotments, because, if within three years of losing his land, he wasn't able to transfer the allotment, he lost it.

Meanwhile, the Agriculture Department was in a dither. They didn't know whether Daddy was legally leasing land with cotton allotments attached or illegally purchasing allotments. In the summer of 1961, they decided to conduct an investigation to try to satisfy themselves as to its legality. During this investigation, they interviewed many of the farmers who had transferred their allotments. By the fall of 1961, Daddy had gotten wind of the investigation. His first reaction was to go to Washington to knock some heads together. This is something Daddy knew how to do very well.

The first man Daddy went to see at the Agriculture Department was Wilson Tucker who was an assistant Director of the Cotton Program. Mr. Tucker later testified at the Senate hearings so we have his version of what occurred, and his description of Daddy's behavior sounds very believable. He said, Daddy, "made vague references to the help he had given the Kenndy election campaign and mentioned the important people he had helped get elected to Washington such as Senator Yarborough. He would make reference to letters from these people which he would pull from his briefcase and start to show me, then would say I didn't need to see them and put them back."

According to Mr. Tucker, Daddy threatened to buy space in New York newspapers and embarrass the whole administration if the investigation into his cotton allotments was not stopped.

At that point, Mr. Tucker wisely referred Daddy to someone higher up in the Department. He sent him to Red Jacobs who managed to calm Daddy down. Mr. Jacobs later had to resign from his post after the Senate committee learned that he went on a shopping spree in Neiman-Marcus in Dallas in the company of Daddy. Jacobs could not convince the committee that Daddy did not pay for the clothes he bought during that trip.

In December of that year, the Agriculture Department completed its investigation and ordered a cancellation of Daddy's 1961 cotton allotments and a suspension of the 1962 allotments. It was mid-winter and the 1961 crop had already been picked and processed and so Daddy would be assessed a fine of about a half million dollars.

Despite this action, Daddy was reappointed to the Cotton Advisory Council. Undersecretary of Agriculture Charles Murphy explained, "The penalty for excess planting was a civil monetary penalty for excess marketing. Many planters overplant, pay the penalty and then are free to market the cotton. The planting of excess cotton by Estes was not a crime. . . ."

When Daddy got word that his allotments had been canceled, he immediately got in touch with Ralph Yarborough who, in turn, got in touch with Murphy and set up a meeting with him for Daddy.

And so Daddy returned to Washington in early 1962. The outcome of his meeting with Murphy was that the cancellation was canceled and Daddy's allotments were reinstated. This simple story proves the importance of having friends in Washington like senators and Vice Presidents. It would be hard to believe that the Agriculture Department would have reconsidered its decision without the intervention of Senator Yarborough.

Within a few short months, Undersecretary Murphy was to regret submitting to the pressures of Senator Yarborough, and Senator Yarborough was, in turn, to deny that he personally knew Daddy.

During the cotton meetings in Washington, a low key but more insidious local investigation was going on. It had been sparked by, of all things, Daddy's desire to serve on the Pecos school board. The people who supported his election were largely people with little or no influence; blacks, Hispanics, and poor whites. The people who opposed him claimed they were against him because of his puritanical views on innocent pleasures such as school dances and mixed bathing. They claimed, if elected, he would succeed in imposing his values on the school.

The real reason they opposed him was because they were afraid that his election would speed integration. In the early sixties in Texas, integration was still a sensitive subject and anyone even vaguely suspected of being for it would be opposed by the local John Birch Society. The owners of the local paper, the *Independent*, were members of the John Birch Society and they vehemently opposed Daddy's election for that reason—and they assured his defeat.

Unfortunately, Daddy, with all his millions, decided to retaliate in the only way he knew how. He decided to start a rival newspaper and put them out of business.

And the owners of the *Independent*, fighting for economic survival, began investigating Daddy's fertilizer tank deals. Their editor won the Pulitzer prize for his series of articles that led to Daddy's arrest. But I'm afraid that the Eastern and national media that lionized the editor for fearless journalism didn't really want to know the paper's real motivation.

V CHAPTER

"Your Daddy's in Jail"

Thursday, March 29, 1962 began as a typical day at our house. In the early evening I came downstairs and found several people in the living room with Mother but thought nothing of it. She said they were having a meeting, and she wanted me to keep the younger children upstairs. We were watching one of our favorite TV shows, "The Real McCoys," when the program was interrupted and a broadcaster said, "Billie Sol Estes has been indicted for fraud and is in the Pecos Jail."

I went downstairs again and people came up to me and said they were sorry Daddy was in jail. I didn't understand what they meant. I began looking for Mother. Another friend came up to me. She was crying. By then, I was upset, too. I found Mother and said, "Mother, is it true Daddy is in jail?"

She started crying and said, "Yes, it's true." I was an eighth grader,

13 years old, and my Daddy was the most wonderful man in the world to me. I just didn't understand how he could be in jail. More friends and relatives arrived during the evening.

Finally, I went to bed, and Mrs. Ben Burns, the wife of the foreman of one of Daddy's farms, came upstairs to be with me. She told me not to worry and to trust in God, that everything would be okay. However, when I woke up Friday, it wasn't just a bad dream. It had really happened.

Friday was the annual "Crazy Day" at Pecos Junior High and everyone came to school in crazy costumes. "Crazy Day" would have been a good name for anyplace in Pecos that day. I was to be mistress of ceremonies at school, so I put on my costume and went to school as if nothing had happened. Wilma, our cook, was supposed to bring fried chicken at noon for the school picnic, but in all the excitement at home, she forgot. I was so confused, I was more upset that Wilma forgot the chicken than because Daddy was in jail. Of course, I was certain it was all a big mistake, and Daddy would be fine.

"Really, this is just a bad dream. I will wake up and he will be home, and everything will be wonderful again." I tried to tell myself, "He has just gone on a business trip." Although I tried to deceive myself with that thought, I knew he was in jail and I would have to begin to face this awful new reality.

Mother kept our house running smoothly even though it was in a state of activity and anxiety. She was confident that "Sol will be okay." Mother recalls the day of the arrest. Daddy had been out of town, arriving back home about 5 p.m. They were in their bedroom, relaxing and reading the paper. Daddy had just taken off his shoes. The cook was preparing dinner and the children were playing. It was to be the last peaceful hour of their lives.

The doorbell rang and the butler, Homer, answered it. It was a U.S. Marshal and he walked into Daddy's bedroom and said, "Mr. Estes, you are under arrest."

Mother says it was the first she knew of any problem. She said Daddy asked, "May I put on my shoes?"

The marshal said, "Yes," and Daddy calmly put on his shoes and went away. Mother went to the telephone and called Uncle John L. Daddy was to spend at least half of the next 20 years in prison, and is still there now.

My brother and sisters and I tried to continue our normal routines. We went to music lessons, church, school and scouts. Many people came to our house to assure us that everything would be okay. Homer went to see Daddy at the jail, and he said he was doing fine. I could not worry about Daddy. I had faith that he would work everything out. No problem was too bad or too big for my Daddy. But I soon realized that this was too big a problem for anybody.

That Friday morning, Homer drove Jan and me, as usual, to junior high school. By that time, everyone knew Daddy was in jail. I was greeted by all my friends, and I tried to have a normal day at school.

We had a boy with behavior problems in our class who was repeatedly pushed from grade to grade by teachers who refused to endure his obnoxious presence for another term. He knew me well because I had tutored him and was one of the few students who had befriended him. Stanley (not his real name) weighed less than 70 pounds and spent the majority of his waking hours picking his nose. When he saw me walk across the school yard, he began yelling, "There's the jail bird's daughter! Your daddy's in jail."

Some of the guys in my class, who were members of the junior varsity football team, picked him up, dropped him in a trash dumpster and closed the steel lid. Despite frantic attempts to get out, Stanley stayed in the dumpster until the end of the day. By then, nearly every student was a co-conspirator in Stanley's confinement. Word spread quickly of Stanley's predicament, but no one told any of the teachers. I was never sure if the big news of the day at Pecos Junior High School was Daddy in jail or Stanley in the dumpster.

Years later, Stanley hitchhiked to Abilene and called Daddy from the Salvation Army. Daddy and I picked him up, bought him some clothes, got him an apartment and found him a maintenance job.

Even though a quiet investigation had been going on for some time, things moved very quickly after the arrest. There were so many investigators that there was a great deal of confusion about what Daddy was supposed to have done.

According to President Kennedy, at one time there were 76 FBI agents working on the case. In Harry Moore's office in Pecos (Moore was the court-appointed receiver), Feds were going over Daddy's records and through his files. Moore said he had six Senate investigators, five men from the FBI and four auditors with 12 more on the way. In addition, a Senate commission was holding a full scale investigation of Daddy's case and the House Government Operations Subcommittee was given about a half a million dollars for investigation expenses.

BY FALL 1962, DADDY HAD BEEN indicted by four grand juries. The grand jury in Pecos brought charges of fraud, and embezzlement. That trial was moved to Tyler. He was indicted in Federal Court in El Paso on the same charges. A federal grand jury in Dallas accused him of making false statements to the Commodity Credit

Corporation. These indictments were later dropped. The fourth was an indictment in Amarillo, accusing him of violating state anti-trust laws for his role in selling fertilizer.

All these indictments resulted in two separate trials. The state tried Daddy in Tyler because an impartial jury could not be found in Pecos.

Soon after the indictments, Attorney General Will Wilson, a candidate for governor of Texas, spoke at a political rally in San Antonio.

He couldn't resist the opportunity to dump on Daddy, saying "Estes Enterprises might wreck the economy of the Texas high plains. He said that Daddy's attempts to corner the grain storage and fertilizer market "had taken all the slack out of the economy of the area."

Wilson said Daddy "was known as a 'Washington operator.' He went to Washington for contracts, money and everything else, tapping into the easy flow of federal money."

He went on to say that Daddy ". . . even had five million bushels of Kansas grain moved into his elevators in Texas, so greedy was he for government contracts. Strange, strange things happen when an operator goes to Washington."

The next day the *Dallas Morning News* reported in a copyrighted story that Daddy was missing. They said even his closest friends and relatives didn't know where he was.

Daddy had attended services at the Church of Christ on Sunday, but reporters had been unable to locate anyone who had seen him since.

Harry T. Moore, federal bankruptcy trustee for Daddy's business operations, also was looking for Daddy. He was supposed to appear in the Court of Inquiry hearings in Pecos. Several of Daddy's friends, including A.B. Foster, were subpoenaed to testify. They went through all proceedings without implicating themselves.

The *Dallas Morning News* story went on to say that rumors were circulating that Daddy had left the country. Giving credence to that story was the fact that my mother also had not been seen since that Sunday church service.

The reason Daddy's original bond was set at the record amount of $500,000 was because Frank Cain, lawyer for one of the finance companies, testified in federal court that Daddy had threatened to go to Brazil, where the U.S. would be unable to extradite him.

The day before, Attorney General Wilson had denied to news reporters that he had any intentions of subpoenaing Daddy for the hearings because he did not want to grant him immunity from prosecution.

Needless to say, Daddy had not run off to Brazil. He continued to believe that he had done nothing wrong and when all the facts had been brought to trial he would be exonerated.

I have often wondered about how different our lives could have been if we would have fled from this country. But where would we have gone? I know Daddy could have started over and maybe we could have even been a family again. But, that is a path we didn't take.

VI CHAPTER

Riches to Rags

I very soon began to get an idea of just how big and bad our problem was. I remained optimistic because I was sure that when Daddy went to trial, everyone would see that he wasn't guilty.

The next year of our lives was occupied almost entirely by trials and hearings. While we kids tried to lead normal lives and attend school each day, Mother and Daddy were constantly on the go. We joined them whenever we could. I think Daddy felt more secure when we were all together.

Mother and Daddy went to great lengths to make us feel safe and secure and not to communicate any anxiety to us. In a way, that made matters worse, because, when Daddy was convicted, it was a great shock to us.

The hearings seemed endless. There were bankruptcy hearings at which Mother had to testify. Attorney General Wilson, who was

BILLIE SOL

Daddy's shown at age 11 with his growing flock. He had started his fortune with a lamb called "Merry."

OPPOSITE PAGE/*Shown here in overalls, on the family farm, Uncle John L. was to often say later of younger brother, Billie, "He's not heavy. . .he's my brother." Their futures were to be very different, but their early close ties were to remain intact.*

TOP PHOTO/*Daddy loved white faced Herefords, and is pictured here with one of his herd. Also pictured is Daddy's younger brother, Bobby.*

AT LEFT/*Shown in this picture, taken by Daddy's mother, Daddy started his fortune with sheep, and had quite a flock by this time when he was 16 years old.*

TOP UPPER LEFT*/Mother had me dressed in my Sunday best ready for church. We never missed a service while we were growing up.*

UPPER RIGHT*/Daddy and Mother and I posed for a snapshot on the porch of our home in Clyde, Texas. I was 2 years old.*

AT LEFT*/Daddy and I looked very happy together here. I was 6 months old.*

OPPOSITE PAGE*/Mother and Daddy were childhood sweethearts and this is their engagement picture taken when Daddy was home on furlough.*

ABOVE/Daddy was selected as one of the top young men of the United States in 1953. Back r L-R: Hiroshi Miyamura, Dr. Lloyd T. Koritz, Maynard Malcolm Miller, W.H. Carter and Dr Albert Schatz. Front row L-R: Daddy, Govern Frank Clement, and Congressman Douglas Stringfellow. Not pictured: Carl T. Rowan, Bis William J. Gordon, Jr.

AT LEFT/In 1960, before the bubble burst, D sat at his desk in his Pecos office, (typically) w foot propped on the desk.

OPPOSITE PAGE TOP PHOTO/One of Da major contributions to agriculture was the natu gas lines he laid making irrigation economically ble for West Texas.

MIDDLE PHOTO/Daddy proudly looks over his thousands of bales of cotton grown in the P area.

BOTTOM PHOTO/This is one of Daddy's pla used in business to fly politicians. His pilot at t time was Frank Crews.

518V
ESTES BROS. FARMS
PECOS, TEXAS

For Billie Sol Estes –
with appreciation and warm regards –
John F. Kennedy

getting ready to run for governor, held a round of hearings and grand jury investigations around the state; that was in addition to the FBI, the IRS, the McClellan Commission, several House committees and the entire media industry.

For the next year we had reporters hanging out of trees. It was tough for them in Pecos because there weren't many trees to hide in. We got to be very adept at running from car to house without getting snapped by a photographer more than once.

There were many people who stood by us, and, of course, some who didn't. Our family was great. They gave us strength and courage. None of them seemed to be embarrassed, just concerned.

In Pecos, many Latin American and black people, whom Daddy had befriended, continued, until we moved to Abilene, to come to our house to bring a few dollars, a sack of fresh vegetables, a bouquet of flowers, a ham or a chicken.

Newspapers, world-wide, were filled with articles. The presses rolled, and we began readjusting to our new lives, which would be an open book from that day on. Daddy's grain elevators were closed. State Agriculture Commissioner, John White, said the state's latest inspection revealed that all Daddy's records were in proper order, and his suspensions were just a precautionary measure.

On April 4, 1962, Daddy turned over to Clayton Anderson and Company the farms he loved and had worked so hard to acquire. They were estimated to be worth about $8 million.

THE SELECTION OF THE AUSTIN FIRM of Cofer and Cofer to represent Daddy's defense was at the insistence of Lyndon Johnson. The subsequent mishandling of the defense by John Cofer, I now believe, was more the result of Cofer's efforts to protect Lyndon

Johnson rather than incompetence.

Cofer was a long-time confidant and representative of Lyndon Johnson. Their relationship went all the way back to Johnson's first election to the U.S. Senate. It was Cofer who represented Johnson in the notorious "Box 13" voter-fraud case in which it was charged that precinct box number 13 in Jim Wells County was tampered with to give Johnson his slim edge that got him elected to the Senate. Cofer remained an important aide to Johnson thereafter.

If we had known at the time about Cofer's relationship to Johnson, it would have been immediately clear why he rested the defense case in both the El Paso and the Tyler trials without calling one single witness. I feel that was done to make sure there was no opportunity of implicating Lyndon Johnson during any testimony or cross examination. It should be clear by now that it was Lyndon Johnson who paved the way for the preferential treatment Daddy received from the Agriculture Department. I don't believe that Johnson wanted Daddy convicted. However, his order of priorities and those of Cofer were, to protect Lyndon Baines Johnson and prevent Daddy's conviction if possible; but, if not, to get the verdict overturned, and, if that didn't work, get Daddy to go to prison all by himself without making any waves. And that is exactly what happened.

One of the most interesting documents I came across in going through the mountains of Daddy's personal papers was Daddy's telephone logs from 1958 up until the big crash. I found it fascinating to chronicle his business activities, day by day, by seeing who he called long distance. These records had been taken from telephone company billing logs. Beginning in 1959, there was a long series of calls to Texas politicians, particularly Ralph Yarborough, and then to Washington. According to the logs, Daddy had a lot of business being conducted with the White House.

LYNDON JOHNSON UNDOUBTEDLY MISSED all that cash he was accustomed to getting from Daddy, but he must have been pleased at how well Mr.Cofer saved him from any embarrassment. Daddy recently remembered one time when he had promised Lyndon a $500,000 contribution but had been slow in sending it. Lyndon called before dawn one morning, "Where the hell is that cash," he bellowed. Daddy replied, "Lyndon, do you know what time it is?"

"Hell, I didn't call you to find out the time. I called you to find out where the hell that cash is. I want you to get out to the fucking airport and get that goddamned cash on its way now." Daddy went on to say, "Lyndon would do anything for you that he could, if you paid him enough."

The Agriculture Department officials, after perjuring themselves at various hearings and trials, must also have felt a great sense of relief that no one called for a Watergate-type investigation after Daddy was convicted. When the dust settled and the score tallied in Washington, there were a few casualties at the Agriculture Department—some firings and resignations, all relatively low-level officials and all for minor transgressions such as accepting gifts of clothes from Daddy.

And, despite the resignations and firings at the Department of Agriculture, there were no indictments. Daddy recently said to me, "Do you really think I'm smart enough to have pulled off all those deals without any help from anyone at the Agriculture Department?"

On the political side, Minnesota Congressman, Carl Andersen, and Texas Congressman, J.T. Rutherford, were defeated for re-election for their association with Daddy, and eventually the voters even nailed Ralph Yarborough. However, despite all the millions of dollars and hundreds of people employed to investigate Daddy, in those pre-Watergate days, no one even paused to consider if some of those elected officials should be in jail with him.

It now appears that in the "Billie Sol Estes" case, John and Robert Kennedy saw an opportunity to get rid of Lyndon Johnson. History has since made clear that they did not want Johnson as vice president and felt he was forced upon them to make sure the Democrats carried the South in the election. They felt that once John Kennedy was the incumbent president, Lyndon Johnson would be of no further use to them, and they could win reelection without him. They began almost immediately manipulating to insure that he would not be on the ticket in 1964. They knew of his great personal unpopularity in Washington political circles. What they hadn't realized was his immense personal political power among the same politicians—both in Washington and in Texas. The politicians would, behind closed doors with the Kennedys, denounce him in graphic and unprintable terms and give the Kennedys the false impression that they wanted to dump Johnson just as much as they did. But when the time came to stand up publicly and be counted, they just weren't there. Robert and John Kennedy realized that it wouldn't be as easy as they thought to get rid of Lyndon Johnson.

The Kennedys did not, of course, instigate the investigation of Daddy's fertilizer tanks. However, when they learned of Daddy's close ties to Lyndon Johnson, they saw an opportunity to publicly humiliate Johnson and rid themselves of him forever, so they threw the full weight of the Justice Department behind the investigation. Why else would the investigation of one man require the full-time efforts of 76 FBI agents?

Lyndon Johnson wasn't about to be ruined by such tactics by two upstarts from Massachusetts. He proved to have more influence than they counted on. In going through all the mounds of trial and investigation testimony, there appeared to be little curiosity about the large cash gifts Daddy had provided for the Democratic Party and Lyndon Johnson personally.

A year and a half later, after John Kennedy was shot while riding down the streets of Dallas in an effort to mend his Texas political ties, Daddy said, "It looks like Lyndon won after all."

DADDY WAS CONVICTED OF CONSPIRACY, as were Harold Orr and Coleman McSpadden. However, justice is very selective. None of the finance company executives had to pay for their part in the "conspiracy," and the charges against the ammonia supplier, Commercial Solvents, were dropped. Daddy's business partner, A.B. Foster, testified for the prosecution but was never indicted. He is now one of the premier citizens of Pecos and has acquired many of Daddy's assets.

THE MOST CURIOUS UNSOLVED MYSTERY of the whole case is the supposed suicide of Henry Marshall, the Agriculture Department official responsible for approving Daddy's cotton allotments. Shortly before the investigations became public, he was found shot to death. His death was ruled a suicide despite the fact that he had been shot in the abdomen five times with a bolt-action rifle—clearly an impossible feat for a suicide. Even after the investigation when his body was exhumed and re-examined, the verdict was left unchanged.

It had been darkly inferred by the investigators and prosecutors that Daddy was somehow responsible for Marshall's death. Federal investigators circulated a composite drawing of an alleged witness wanted for questioning in the Marshall case that had an uncanny resemblence to Daddy. They claimed the man in the drawing had asked directions to Marshall's farm shortly before Marshall was shot—not an intelligent act for a man intending to commit murder.

THE EVENTS THAT LED TO DADDY'S downfall seem to echo two recurring themes that blinded Daddy and his friends to reality. One was the feeling that he was invincible and that he and his friends in Washington were all-powerful and could fix anything, and the other was that whatever Daddy did would automatically work and was insured from failure. Going back to the time Daddy decided to branch out from farming and get into other agriculture-related businesses, it's easy to see now, in retrospect, how it all came tumbling down.

At that time, one of the most attractive agriculture-related businesses was anhydrous ammonia fertilizer. Daddy already spent a great deal each year putting anhydrous ammonia into the ground, using portable tanks. He had bought the local farm implement and supply business as farmers were following his lead and beginning to irrigate and fertilize.

It was clear that the fertilizer business was going to be a high growth business and so he decided to corner the market in West Texas. There were already a number of dealers in the plains area in the Panhandle where farmers had been irrigating for a number of years. He quickly took his fertilizer sales from zero to over a million dollars a year.

In 1958 Daddy went to New York to visit his ammonia supplier, Commercial Solvents, and made them a bold proposal. He asked Commercial Solvents to lend him close to a million dollars, most of which would go to wipe out his accounts payable with them, but a quarter of a million would go for a down payment on a grain storage facility. Daddy would assign the receipts from the storage facility to them as security for the loan. It was attractive security because receipts to the facility were from government contracts, which was like money in the bank. Daddy had already begun making large political contributions to LBJ, so future storage contracts at other facilities were also like money in the bank.

Commercial Solvents liked the arrangement, and for reasons other than the fact that they had their accounts receivable secured. Daddy had announced his intention of cornering the fertilizer market, and, to do this, he intended to sell anhydrous ammonia at below cost until all ammonia dealers in West Texas were working for him. He would, in fact, be subsidizing the expansion of Commerical Solvents. He very quickly became their largest customer.

Daddy also very quickly became the largest distributor of anhydrous ammonia in the world. As he predicted, most of the dealers ended up working for him. His fertilizer sales contracts also gave him an edge in getting grain storage business from the farmers who were buying the ammonia. In addition to subsidizing his supplier, he was also subsidizing the farmers who were getting their fertilizer at below manufacturers' cost. The fertilizer was also producing larger grain crops and hence more business for grain storage facilities.

The drawback to all this was the cost of the fertilizer subsidy Daddy was providing for Commercial Solvents and to the farmers. At this point, Daddy began to need additional financing to maintain his "gameplan." He had always been able to borrow large sums of money. Like any successful businessman, he believed the secret of getting rich was the ability to maintain a reasonable profit margin on borrowed money—the more money employed, the more profit, so he looked around for new avenues of borrowing.

It was then that he hit on the idea of "buying" other people's credit. There is nothing shady nor dishonest about the idea of using other people's credit to make purchases for which you pay them a fee, but such credit was expensive because, not only was he paying the interest on the "purchased" credit, but he was also paying a fee to the co-signer for the use of his credit, thus paying interest twice.

The finance companies liked this plan. It would provide Daddy the cash he needed and allow them to purchase the paper at a very attractive discount. They would be making about 40% on their investment.

This is the way it would work: The farmer whose credit was being "purchased" would buy fertilizer tanks from Superior Manufacturing Company and sign a mortgage for the purchase price. He would not pay out any cash. Daddy would in turn lease the tank from the farmer, making the lease payment directly to Superior Manufacturing, i.e. the finance company that had purchased the mortgage, and then would pay the farmer a 10 percent fee.

The only catch was that there were not enough fertilizer tanks. Superior Manufacturing was not able to keep up with production demands. What the situation came to was that Daddy was borrowing money with just the farmers as co-signers and no other security. Had there been no investigation, the loan repayments would have continued until the debt was retired and there would have been no scandal.

The finance companies, greedy for their 40 percent discount, agreed to look the other way when taking the tank inventory because they believed in Daddy's Midas touch just like everybody

else. He had never lost any money for anyone before that time.

ONE OF THE THINGS I HAVE BEEN hearing since then is how unfortunate it was for all the farmers who lost all that money when they could ill afford to. I have since discovered, by going through court records, Daddy's bankruptcy hearing transcripts, and many other documented sources, that none of those farmers lost anything beyond the bonuses Daddy paid them. In fact, even those who had to repay the bonus didn't pay back all of it. It is also not true that they were conned into co-signing.

Uncle John L. tells me that at about that time he was in Pecos, and there were people lined up outside Daddy's office waiting to "get in on the tank deal." Some of them were collecting $40,000 to $50,000 for co-signing.

Some were undoubtedly motivated by the chance to make some easy money; some were convinced that if Daddy was doing it, it must be all right; and at least one man, if you can believe his testimony, was doing it because he wanted to help Daddy. Long after the trials were over and Daddy was in jail and nobody had anything to gain from lying; in fact, in 1967 at one of the endless bankruptcy hearings, Mr. Will H. Weaver, in response to questioning by Allan Poage, attorney of the bankruptcy trustee, stated: "There'd be years down there when I'd come up with owing three or four thousand dollars (to Daddy). All right, I just didn't have it. All right, I'd go and tell Estes and he'd say, 'Well, ain't nobody pushing you are there Weaver?' I'd say, 'No sir.' He'd say, 'Well, when you get the money, pay me.' And that's the way we operated and maybe I wouldn't pay him until nearly fall but I always went in and paid the bill. . . ."

"I had a farm that was thirty miles south of Pecos. He had a small farm not far away. It had sixty-eight acres on it and I went in to lease the farm from him . . . I believe the appointment was for ten thirty so I went in and asked him if he would lease me this land. I says 'its's a sore thumb in your side, it's a way out of your operation.' He says, 'Why don't you come back at ten thirty Thursday?' He says, 'I have no appointments, and I think I could lease you that piece of land.' "

And then Mr. Weaver very matter-of-factly said something curious. Four years previously at Daddy's trials, all the finance companies had denied any prior knowledge of Daddy's tank leasing operation. Weaver continued his testimony, saying, "Thursday at ten thirty I come back in and go in Mr. Estes office and he introduced me to this . . . oh, the head man of C.I.T. out of Dallas."

When Poage asked him if he meant Mr. Kerr, Weaver replied, "Well, the one that he had in his hip pocket. Nothing ever come up about the farm. He said, 'Bill, I need a little help,' and I said, 'Well, Estes, how can I help you?' I said, 'I'm broke now and I can't help you.' He said, 'Well, you have a financial statement don't you?" I said, 'Yeah, such as it is any more.' He said, 'Well,' he said, 'you owed me a little money down through the years and I never pushed you for payment since you've never missed paying me.' So he says 'I've got my back against the wall and I need some help.' So I says, 'What kind of help can I give you, Estes?'

About this time, the C.I.T. man spoke up. He said, 'Mr Weaver,' he said, 'Estes' credit is extended,' and he said, 'we know what he's doing. If you want to go along with him and loan him your financial statement, we will loan him enough money to buy some tanks on your financial statement.' I said, 'That's not a very good deal, I don't think, because I got, you know, most of my financial statement up with Western Cotton Oil,' and I told him, I said, 'Well, and, too, it sounds kind of funny.' I says, 'You don't get nothing for nothing.' I says, 'There's an old rule about that.' He says, 'Well, Mr. Weaver,' says, 'if you loan him sixty-nine thousand dollars,' he says . . . So, I said, 'I won't go for it. I'll have to go talk to my people.'

"So I went and talked to Western cotton Oil about it and they said, 'Well I don't see why. Everybody else is on it.' . . . and I needed twenty-five hundred dollars to make two tractor payments, so I took the twenty-five hundred. I went over and talked to an income-tax man and got my statements all filled out, my financial statement. . . ."

Weaver goes on to tell how the lease and mortgage payments were set up. His bonus money was paid up front. Every month the lease payment, which was equivalent to the mortgage payment, was made, and Mr. Weaver would send a check to the finance company from a special account he had set up. Daddy did not miss any lease payments until the crash that April.

Not only did Mr. Weaver testify that Daddy never missed a lease payment, but so did twenty or thirty others during the bankruptcy proceedings at various times. That certainly contradicts the contention of the IRS that the tank leases were not loans but simple taxable income.

The principal investigator for the IRS was Aubrey J. Drew who made a deposition in 1966 relating to Daddy's bankruptcy. When asked the nature and scope of his work on the Billie Sol Estes case he replied, "I was assigned to the Billie Sol Estes case in July or August of 1962. I was assigned initially as a criminal investigator, and my principal work included the determination of the amount of money Estes had received from selling or discounting anhydrous ammonia equipment contracts, contracts on which I found no security existed as described on the contracts, and which resulted in considerable amounts of swindle income to Billie Sol Estes."

The audit lasted from early 1962 to early 1966. When asked how many man hours were spent on this audit and investigation he replied, "Five agents for a period of approximately four years."

Mr. Drew waffled when asked about the general accuracy of Daddy's accounts. However, when pressed, he did admit that they conformed to generally accepted standards. He was determined though, to see in them what he wanted to see. He was asked by Mr. Poage, "Were these books that you just described comparable to other books of account that you have seen during other audits that you have performed for the United States Government?"

He replied, "I would say that mathematically they were comparable to most of the records I have seen. However, they contained entries which were highly unusual in comparison with other businesses I had examined."

He was asked to explain. "As far as the method of keeping the records on the double entry method and maintaining journals and related control and subsidiary accounts from a mathematical point of view, they were relatively accurate."

Mr. Drew went on to complain that because collateral for loans was missing, the amounts shown on the books as notes payable were swindle income. Mr. Poage questioned him further, "Mr. Drew, I gather that all these transactions that you are just now telling us about were recorded on Mr. Estes' books, were they not?"

"Yes. Yes they were."

"And I take it from your answer that your dispute is a classification under which they were recorded, is that correct?"

"Well, my interpretation is that this money as it was received, there was nothing in the records to show that it was a loan to Estes. . . ."

"Well, if you had to characterize Mr. Estes' books compared

generally with other books of account that you had seen, would you classify them as below average, average or above average?"

At this point, the attorney representing the IRS jumped in, "Mr. Poage, what do you mean by classifying? Mr. Drew has already said that entries were made that weren't supported by documents. What do you mean by this classification? I don't think I understand your question."

There ensued a lively argument in which Mr. Poage repeated the question and the IRS attorney objected. Finally Mr. Drew had to admit, "From a mathematical point of view and the fact that the books generally were in balance, the figures added up correctly, but the classification and the recording of transactions on records in my opinion were not correct with regard to the amounts received from selling or discounting anhydrous ammonia equipment contracts."

Mr. Poage: Mr. Drew, would you just answer the question, please, as was put? Would you describe the Estes books compared with other books that you have seen as below average or average or above average?

Mr. Fradkin: (attorney for IRS) I think Mr. Drew has sufficiently answered that question.

Mr. Poage: You won't let him answer that? You have your objection in.

Mr. Fradkin: Mr. Poage, I am not objecting at this point because he already answered. He said the books didn't have supporting documents for certain answers. . . . I think he has sufficiently answered it.

Mr. Poage: Mr. Drew, you talked about the tank transactions. I will ask you whether or not Mr. Estes recorded on his books the cash received and the result of these transactions?

Mr. Drew: Yes, he did.

Mr. Poage: Did he not record those transactions on his books as liabilities?

Mr. Drew: That's right.

Mr. Poage: Did Mr. Estes record on his books tank transactions in which he in effect did not receive any money?

Mr. Drew: Yes, he did.

Mr. Poage: Did he reflect these transactions on his books as liabilities?

To this repeated question throughout the proceeding, Mr. Drew reluctantly answered a very, very qualified yes. It was the IRS's contention that, even though these transactions were being carried on Daddy's books as loans, and even though Daddy was making current payments on them as loans up until the time of his bankruptcy, in fact, those transactions were "swindle income" and, as such, were subject to taxation, regardless of whether or not Daddy had actually gotten the money.

Another generally held misconception since the crash in March of 1962 was that there were no anhydrous ammonia tanks. While it is true that there were many missing tanks, it always appears more monstrous and sinister to say there were *no* tanks. It makes better newspaper reading and better courtroom drama. There are two irrefutable sources of rebuttal to the charge that there were no tanks. One is the annual accounts payable to Commercial Solvents for more than $3,000,000 for ammonia which requires tanks in order to be dispensed. The other source of rebuttal is the reluctant testimony of Mr. Drew in the same hearing. He is questioned by Mr. Lynch, representative of the finance companies. Mr. Fradkin is the government attorney, his counsel:

Mr. Lynch: . . . Estes enterprises did have substantial numbers of anhydrous ammonia tanks, did it not?
Mr. Fradkin: What do you mean by substantial?
Mr. Lynch: If the witness does not understand my question, I would like for him to say so.
Mr. Fradkin: No, I am asking you.

Mr. Fradkin: Mr. Lynch, I am asking you to clarify your question. . . . Something substantial to you might not be substantial to my witness.
Mr. Lynch: I want the record to show that in almost every instance. . . .
Mr. Fradkin: No, I will object to what you are saying.

Mr. Lynch: Well, I am going to say it whether you object to it or not—that the witness is being prompted by counsel.
Mr. Fradkin: I will object to your saying prompted, Mr. Lynch.
Mr. Lynch: Being whispered to by counsel without the witness asking for any help from counsel. I feel that this witness has a vast knowledge of this case and I would like to get his testimony rather than counsel's.
Mr. Fradkin: Mr. Lynch, you are not getting my testimony. My client has a right to confer with me at any time.
Mr. Lynch: I can't see that he is asking for any conference. You are volunteering suggestions to him while we are trying to interrogate him.
Mr. Fradkin: I am glad that you can tell what I am doing, Mr. Lynch. I am glad that you are a mind reader. All I am asking you to do at this point is define your questions more specifically. I am sorry that you are getting. . . .
Mr. Lynch: Will the witness answer the question, please?
Mr. Drew: Estes records showed that he had some tanks, but I am not sure that I know what would be meant by a substantial number of tanks.

They never did determine how many tanks Daddy had—or did not have.

Mr. Drew then testified as to the amount of net taxable income which resulted from these transactions. For 1960, he figured that Daddy owed tax on $4,197,919.88. For 1961, the figure was $10,959,991.28. It's no wonder that people thought Daddy had money salted away in Switzerland. The fact is, as shown later in the testimony, most of that money went to pay off the mortgages on the nonexistent as well as existing tanks. I recently asked Daddy what he was planning to do with all that money he was borrowing. "I was going to build more grain storage facilities," he said.

Toward the end of Mr. Drew's testimony, Jack Bryant, who was representing Daddy at that time (this was in 1967) managed to get in one good question:

Mr. Bryant: Do you have any personal knowledge or any knowledge based on reports that you have seen that would identify the two men who, during the course of October, and November and December of 1963 maintained a telephone tap on the. . . .

Mr. Fradkin: Now, I will. . . .

Mr. Bryant: Just a minute. If he doesn't know anything, I just want him to say so. Off the record a minute.

(Whereupon an off-the-record discussion was had.)

Mr. Bryant: In your position in the Intelligence Section of the Internal Revenue and your connection with this case, do you have any knowledge of any telephone taps maintained by the Internal Revenue Service at any time since October of 1963 on the telephones in the home of Billie Sol Estes at 70 Castle Drive, Abilene, Texas, on my office in the Petroleum Building, Abilene, Texas, on the office of J.L. Estes, Jr. on North 19th Street in Abilene, Texas?

Mr. Drew naturally denied knowledge of the telephone taps.

VII CHAPTER

Tribulations and Trials

I firmly believe that if Daddy had been operating out of a big city like Houston or Dallas, the tank financing scheme would have perked right along until the debt was retired and it would be obscure financial history. Daddy, and the farmers, and the finance companies would all have made money and everybody would have been happy and moved on to something else.

However, since Daddy operated out of Pecos, everybody knew everything about everybody else. In a small town whenever somebody records a deed or mortgage at the courthouse, some busybody will always know about it, and soon everybody in town will know. In this case, the newspaper that was rival to Daddy's newspaper, the *Pecos Daily News*, began its crusade against Daddy and sparked the investigation.

A local doctor, John Dunn, who was one of the owners of the

rival paper was also head of the local branch of the John Birch Society. He contended that Daddy's views on integration and democratic politics in general were detrimental to the future of the Republic. At his prodding, the newspaper started a vendetta that resulted in Daddy's downfall.

Well, with a full-fledged investigation under way, it wasn't long until the Agriculture Department decided to decertify Daddy's storage facilities, not because they knew of any wrongdoing, as they themselves admitted, but "just in case." With the loss of government contracts, all of which were spotlessly legitimate even if they did come courtesy of LBJ, there was no way payments could be made on all the loans. In that event it stands to reason that either the lender or the co-signer must take the loss.

At that point, there was a sufficient amount of press hysteria to make the most innocent business deal look sinister. While Daddy's deals were far from being innocent, many people who had profited from association with Daddy—almost the whole town of Pecos—were ready to defend him, *as long as there were no losses*, as the man who brought prosperity to Pecos. However, when the losses began, many of those people deserted him and jumped on the band wagon to "hang it all on Billie Sol."

Regardless of Daddy's good intentions, of his charity, of his Midas touch, his borrowings through Superior Manufacturing could not stand close legal scrutiny.

Unless he was willing to testify and seek immunity in order to implicate government officials, finance company officials, and Commercial Solvent executives, he was bound to go to jail. His trial was simply a confirmation of that fact. Still, Daddy stubbornly refused to testify.

At the trials, the farmers who co-signed the notes swore that they didn't know what they were doing, that their signatures were forgeries, and that they were pressured into signing. I can't remember an instance when I've heard of anyone co-signing a loan against his will, yet all those farmers who had made lots of money when Daddy helped make their farms more productive now said they just "flat didn't know what made them do it."

Likewise at the trials, the finance companies claimed to have had no idea there were no fertilizer tanks. They said they were deceived by the cleverest swindler who ever came down the pike. They thought the reason they were getting the paper at such a ridiculously favorable discount was because Daddy didn't know any better.

Several years after Daddy went to jail and long after the media had lost interest in the story of the "poor farmers who had lost so much money," a group of farmers, headed by a Mr. Barnes, sued Daddy (actually Daddy's bankrupt estate) and several of the finance companies including the Walter Heller Company of Chicago. The suit charged that the farmers had been defrauded by Daddy and the finance companies. The jury found both the farmers and the finance companies had acted in bad faith and refused to award them damages. Furthermore, the appeals court assessed the farmers and the finance companies $81,000 and awarded it to Harry Moore, Daddy's bankruptcy trustee, to help defray court costs in the case.

In addition to that, the case was heard in Pecos, the home of most of the farmers who supposedly had been defrauded.

I don't want to be Pollyann-ish about Daddy's involvement in this debacle or even about his capability, but I would like to clarify it and tell the story in simple straightforward terms.

I've already told about how Daddy got rich by introducing irrigation and fertilizer to the Pecos area. Well, it's not hard to figure out that many other people got rich right along with him for the very same reasons. Maybe not *as* rich, but certainly rich. After all, if he increased the productivity and value of his own land fourfold, then the value and productivity of his neighbor's land was increased right along with it.

Before Daddy came to Pecos there were some farmers who were already irrigating, but they found it a very chancy and expensive operation because of the cost of electricity for pumping the water. Most farmers had shied away from irrigation for that reason.

Daddy knew that there was plenty of cheap natural gas in the area that could be used to drive the irrigation pumps and eliminate the major disadvantage to irrigating. The only problem was that the nearest gas pipeline was 40 miles away.

Daddy was responsible for bringing that pipeline to within reach of each farmer in the county, thus completely rebuilding the farm economy in that area.

The difference between these people and Daddy was that Daddy was a risk-taker. When he first irrigated, he was taking a calculated risk that could have ruined him if any number of negative things had happened. For example, if the irrigation wells had produced overly mineralized water, if the reservoirs had been smaller than calculated, Daddy would have lost his investment. The people who copied him were not taking a risk since they did not make an investment in irrigation until Daddy proved that it was feasible. The same thing was true for fertilization.

Many people in the area had come to believe that Daddy had a magic touch and that whatever Billie Sol Estes did would make money. They were wrong. It was not magic that made Daddy's schemes work but intelligently calculated risks. The important factor that people overlooked was that no matter how intelligently calculated, they were still risks. That fact became the basis of the problem. When Daddy asked farmers to sell him their credit by going on paper for fertilizer tanks, he was asking them to take a calculated risk. They did so willingly, though obviously not because they thought they were going to lose their money. However, they unfortunately had come to believe that an investment with Billie Sol Estes was a guarantee to make money, so therefore, a loss must be fraud.

This was the kind of risk Daddy took all the time, and everybody who knew him understood that. When the risks paid off, Daddy was a hero because he had made them lots of money. If the risk failed, they ran for cover. That's exactly what they did.

THE HEARINGS AND TRIALS TENDED to distort rather than clarify Daddy's operations for several reasons. One reason for that is the rules of evidence in court allow only a very narrow version of any event or situation, stripping away extenuating or mitigating circumstances that could alter the meaning of an event or action. Another reason is that witnesses are most often self-serving, trying to save their own skins. In almost all cases in Daddy's trials, the witnesses were people who had been granted immunity from indictment. In exchange, they had to promise to help convict Daddy.

And finally, there is the coloration given to the events by the news media, whose goals are to sell newspapers or magazines.

To cite just one example, *Life* magazine on June 1, 1962 printed an article by Richard Dulahan, stating the reason for Daddy's defeat in the school board election was, "Billie Sol ran on a platform that called for a ban on all dancing and segregation of drinking fountains so that boys and girls would not drink together at school. 'We could put up with him running every business in town, and mortgaging our homes and all that,' says a Pecos housewife, 'but when it comes to meddling in our children's lives, we drew the line.' "

In the first place, in small town school board elections, there are no platforms, the candidates run on their reputation and call on voters to elect them as their friend. In the second place, Daddy had a reputation of socializing with blacks and Mexicans and favoring integration. In Texas in the early 60s any hint of integrating schools was enough for lesser people than Daddy to be ostracised. If Daddy had had a platform, it would have been to integrate schools. *Life* magazine made no mention of that possibility. They did not want a balanced story, they wanted to create a specific bias. And they were very good at it.

The news reporters, when they came to Pecos and saw a rich irrigated prosperous farming industry, either did not know or did not choose to know that Daddy was almost single-handedly responsible for turning it from a semi-arid desert to the lush cropland they were seeing.

From the time he was arrested, he was cast as a villain; and the media was consistent in their portrayal of him as such. This early reporting colored the hearings and the trials and influenced all the motions for appeal.

Much is made of moving trials in order to assure impartial juries, while the need for impartial judges is almost totally ignored. If anything, getting an impartial judge is much more difficult and critical to whether or not a trial is fair and impartial than getting an unbiased jury. An impartial jury can very quickly be swayed by a biased judge who knows how to manipulate a jury.

I think Daddy's case is an excellent example of this. The subtleties of judge-to-jury influence are hard to pinpoint and cannot be discovered just by reading trial transcripts, making it hard to base an appeal on judicial partiality as John Cofer did. The very tone of voice a judge uses when addressing the jury can convey a meaning exactly opposite to the words coming out of his mouth, which are taken down and become part of the transcript for the record, proving to the appeals court that the judge said nothing prejudicial to the jury. If the judge is contemptuous or flippant, that fact does not go into the transcript, but the jury still gets the message. There's little question in the minds of the jurors about how the judge wants them to vote.

AT NEITHER THE TYLER NOR THE El Paso trial would Mr. Cofer, Daddy's attorney, confer with him. We, at first, thought that at the end of each day, Daddy would meet with Cofer to review what was happening or what their next day's strategy would be. During the proceedings, Daddy would frequently lean over the table to whisper to Mr. Cofer when he heard a particular bit of testimony and perhaps say to him, "That testimony can be refuted by Mr. Blank," or, "The answer to that question just asked by the prosecution is in such and such a document." Mr. Cofer would ignore him.

Mother and Daddy didn't press him to listen or accept the information Daddy was giving him because they had always thought that lawyers were a lot like surgeons, and you didn't question what they were doing even if it didn't seem to make sense to a layman. Uncle John L. and Mother talked several times about firing Cofer, but it didn't seem like a wise move because the trial had started, and besides, they had already given him the last of Daddy's money.

In recalling the trials, Mother said recently, "We felt in our hearts he was mishandling the trials, but since never in our lives had we had any experience with courts, we trusted him as the professional expert. Besides, he had been recommended by Lyndon Johnson and that gave us confidence."

Actually there were a few times that Cofer talked to us. One such time was to explain why he wasn't going to introduce evidence that the finance companies knew that there were no fertilizer tanks, "The reason," he said, "is because if we prove that the finance companies knew about the tanks, then we just make you look more guilty."

He neglected to mention that if he could prove that the finance companies knew that there were no fertilizer tanks, there was no fraud. The prosecution clearly knew this and indicated as much by the witnesses they chose from the finance companies. In normal trial procedure, the prosecution would call those executives who had been directly responsible for negotiating the loans, but they did not. They called executives from the home offices of the companies who could truthfully say, when asked if they knew what was going on, that they did not.

Another puzzling thing John Cofer did was during jury selection at the Tyler trial. Understandably, he wanted to select an unbiased jury, and yet, he ended up with a largely biased jury. How did he do it? He began, as we've all seen on TV, by asking prospective jurors if they had ever heard of Billie Sol Estes, or if they had read about the case in the newspapers, seen reports of it on TV, or heard from family or friends what it was all about. At that time almost 100 per cent of even marginally educated and aware people, or people who might have shared Daddy's values and could have sympathized with a self-made millionaire, were automatically excluded because they or their families routinely read newspapers or watched the news on TV.

That means that his selection process would tend to favor people on the jury who might be ignorant, uninformed, and perhaps prejudiced against anyone who was ambitious and successful.

Then came the curious part of his questioning. Having excused everybody who had heard or read about the case, and, satisfied that he had a totally uninformed individual on his hands, he then brought out a wanted poster, prepared by one of our government agencies, of a man purporting to be a witness wanted in connection with the death of Henry Marshall. The so-called composite drawing of that witness had an uncanny resemblence to Daddy. He proceeded to ask each prospective juror if he or she had ever seen that wanted poster, thus planting a suggestion in the minds of the jurors that Daddy might also be wanted for murder. If he had just left the matter alone he could have been assured that none of the jurors had ever heard of the death of Henry Marshall and that he was only making them suspicious by even bringing up the matter.

I have agonized many times since then about what could have been going on in his mind or what he thought he was doing. Now that I am grown up and writing a book about it, I would love to be able to call him on the phone and ask him. I can't do it because John Cofer is dead. The only charitable excuse for him I can think of is that he thought, perhaps, if he could succeed in showing that an unbiased jury could not be found in Tyler, he could get the trial moved once again and eventually wear down the prosecution until they gave up trying to prosecute Daddy. In retrospect, that would have been the most unrealistic strategy he could have used.

By the time we got to the end of the trial, Mother and Uncle John L. were too numb to protest when he rested the defense case *without calling any witnesses,* intending to win the case with his summation alone. Even though I was only an adolescent, I knew that something was terribly wrong with that. We had listened to more than a month of prosecution testimony during which Daddy was called every name I had ever heard and a few that were new to me. I knew that he was entitled to a defense and that he was not given one.

The only part of the Tyler trial that Cofer handled correctly in my view was the appeal. He based the appeal on the circus-like atmosphere caused by the presence of TV cameras and won. Cofer had protested the presence of cameras at the beginning of the trial. He argued that it would create a circus, but he was overruled. Judge Dunagan said that television was part of the news media. "I can see no justifiable reason why it should not take its seat in the family circle. . . ." "Family circus" would have been a more apt description.

He went on to say, "I have encountered no difficulty with television in previous cases, and I have been unable to observe any distraction of the witnesses or others." At the noon recess the first day of the trial, he had told the press, "There is always a possibility the high court may disagree." Fortunately for Daddy, it did.

Cofer's behavior at the El Paso trial was very little different from what it was at the Tyler trial. But, of course, the results were similar. Daddy was found guilty. It took the jury somewhat longer, and twice they came back deadlocked and desperately wanted the judge to excuse them from any further deliberation. The judge, at that point, reminded them that the government had spent more than a million dollars on this trial, and said, "I'm not going to waste it on a mistrial."

With such a clear message to the jury, by now exhausted, wanting to go home, and probably hating each other, Daddy, the judge, and all the attorneys, it's not really surprising that they went back into the jury room and came back with a guilty verdict.

The judge's remarks to the jury after they asked to be dismissed are what lawyers call a "dynamite charge," so-called because it is used to break up a "log jam" in a jury room whenever a deadlock occurs. The Supreme Court has been inconsistent in its rulings on "dynamite charges," overturning verdicts in some cases and upholding others.

John Cofer based his appeal in the El Paso case on the Judge's "dynamite charge" to the jury and that appeal was denied, not only by the U.S. Court of Appeals in New Orleans, but also by the Supreme Court.

The charge to the jury that Cofer objected to follows. It was given by the judge after the jury reported that it was hopelessly deadlocked. It says in part:

On March 27, 1963 at 3:40 P.M., the Court called the jury into the courtroom and gave them the following additional charge:

"Ladies and Gentlemen of the jury: The Court has received the following note from your foreman, Mr. Robbin E. L. Washington, which reads as follows: 'By common consent, this jury has decided that we cannot reach a verdict in this case'; so the Court has called you in to just have a frank and honest discussion with you about that situation. The Court would like to say first of all, however, that he doesn't want and instructs every member of the jury not to say how you stand numerically, he is not interested in that, he will not ask the question himself, and he requests that none of you say how you stand numerically. Now, the Court, as he hopes you have found out, tries to be courteous and considerate to all the officers of the Court, not only the lawyers in the case and witnesses who may testify, but especially the members of the jury because you are officers of this court. Now, the Court regrets that you are, in your opinion, at the moment at least unable to agree upon a verdict, and I would like to explore the matter a little, though, to make sure there is no chance for you to arrive at a fair and just verdict based on the law and the

evidence. This case, as you know, has consumed now two and a half weeks, it has been a hotly contested case with many witnesses and much testimony. You have heard the argument of the lawyers and the charge of the Court covering the law, and the Court would like to say by way of compliment that the evidence shows that you worked hard on trying to arrive at a verdict for the last thirty hours. *You went to your jury room yesterday morning at eleven o'clock and you have been kept together ever since except during a few hours of sleep last night. You have worked diligently today, and as evidence of the fact that you have been on the job and working in an honest effort to arrive at a verdict, you have written the Court several notes regarding various aspects of his charge on the law of the case which the Court has tried to promptly and properly answer.* This, as you know, is a very important case, not only to the Government of the United States, but especially to this defendant. Cases in this country of ours have to be tried sometime by somebody, and verdicts have to sometime be agreed upon, if that is possible. In other words, cases have to be decided one way or the other in order that they may be disposed of. This has been an expensive trial to the Government and to the defendant too, and, of course, the Government's expenses are paid by the taxpayers, which includes you, so it is important that every reasonable and proper effort be given an honest jury to try to arrive at a verdict, if that is possible or probable. *The Court doesn't say it to flatter you, but* he knows you are fine, patriotic, law-abiding, good honest citizens of high integrity who have great regard for your oaths and want to do your duty as you see it. The Court wants it very strictly understood that whatever conclusion we may reach in a few minutes, the Court doesn't want anybody to surrender or compromise any of his or her convictions that he or she conscientiously holds. We don't want any compromise verdict, but we don't want a verdict where there is any coercion by the majority on the minority if you are divided unequally, we just want you as honest, patriotic, law-abiding citizens under your oaths to determine the guilt or innocence of this defendant and do it independently on your own judgement.

It seems to me that the judge was sending a very mixed message to the jury, mixed in favor of forcing a decision to break the deadlock. The judge repeats over and over again that "The important thing . . . is that the case has to be tried sometime by somebody and a verdict must be arrived at and (I) want to give you that opportunity." In other words, the judge is going to sit on them until they reach a verdict. The judge tries to cloak this instruction in a mass of verbiage. He goes on:

Sometimes, of course, people can talk things over and argue questions out to where they do reach an agreement that is satisfactory to all and also retain their judgment but above all their conscientious beliefs. The Court repeats that under no circumstances would he intimate or stand for anybody surrendering his or her conscientious belief about the merits of this case, whether it be for conviction or acquittal. The important thing, ladies and gentlemen, is that, as the Court said a moment ago, the case has to be tried sometime by somebody and a verdict arrived at by twelve fair and impartial jurors such as I know you to be, but if there is any reasonable opportunity or probability that by further conferring you might agree on a verdict, the Court wants to give you that opportunity. *You have discussed the matter at some length I am sure during your thirty hours of deliberation, you have discussed the case from many standpoints, if you have such fixed opinion that you are certain that you cannot agree on a fair and impartial verdict while at the same time retaining your conscientious convictions on the matter,* why then, of course, the Court will discharge you and order a new trial. *Now then, the Court has to leave it very largely to you, he just wants to be of aid and assistance to you, if you think by further deliberation you might be able to agree on a verdict, and he repeats that he doesn't want to know how you stand numerically, and regardless of how you stand, there is to be no coercion or insistence on anybody in the minority giving up their conscientious beliefs and convictions, you will retain those to the last, but if you do think and believe that by further consideration and deliberation you might be able to arrive at a verdict in a reasonable time, the Court wants to give you that opportunity. He repeats too that you are officers of the court, you have shown that you have taken your duties very seriously, you realize that you are under oath to try the case according to the law and the evidence and to return a verdict on that and nothing else; and that is the only kind of a verdict the court wants or would accept. So, now, he just has to leave it in your hands and then the Court try to arrive at a fair conclusion as to whether or not it is worthwhile to continue further deliberations. How do you feel about it, Mr. Foreman?" (Emphasis added)*

A discussion followed between the Court and the members of the jury. Mr. Gutierrez said: "Your Honor, I think we went through this as much as possible and it was deadlocked because, as you mentioned at the beginning, some of us didn't want to change what we thought it was our sincere verdict in our discussion, and that is why it is deadlocked."

Mrs. Carter said: "Your Honor, I don't think that if we stayed there for a week that it would do any good."

Nine of the jurors said they were willing to try some more.

The Court then said:

"Well, now, the Court repeats that he just wants to be fair and

frank and honest with you just like you are being with him, he repeats this case has to be tried, decided sometime by somebody by some jury in some way. This Court is not interested in doing anything except trying to administer justice and get verdicts, but — you talk a lot about the jury system in this country, but if they don't arrive at verdicts, it doesn't work, the jury system is a failure in that particular case at least if the jury doesn't arrive at a verdict, so the Court feels in all fairness to all parties he ought to give you another chance inasmuch as I believe the majority of you . . . would be willing to make some further effort, is that right (all jurors answered in the affirmative), everybody is willing to try it again.

In other words, if you don't bring in a verdict, you are all failures in your civic duty and not the kind of sterling citizens this court is used to dealing with.

Well, now, let the Court again say to you that he is not trying to coerce you, he wouldn't do it if he could, or to use a slang expression, he is not trying to put any heat on you, he instructs you very definitely that ur are not to surrender your conscientious convictions, you are not to reach a verdict by compromise, you are to talk over the facts in this case, the evidence as presented here from the witness stand, and the law that the Court gave you, and he repeats he has been glad to answer your questions the best he could, but in view of the fact that it is a very important case, and long and complicated, he has given you the law the best he understands it with his limitations, so the Court could not improve upon the charge he gave you, he tried to read it to you clearly and distinctly, and you know I think what it contains." (Emphasis added)

And then added:

"Well, if there are any exhibits that were offered in evidence, the Court will see that the Clerk consults with the attorneys and the

Court Reporter and send them to you. So, ladies and gentlemen, the Court very much appreciates your fine attitude. He is going to give you a reasonable time to talk some more. He repeats he is not going to punish you by just holding you, if it becomes absolutely apparent that there is no hope of you reaching a verdict, but if you do think you can reach a verdict based on the law and the evidence and nothing else, and following your conscientious convictions and your best judgment, *the Court would appreciate your trying to arrive at a verdict.* Thank you very much, you will go back and resume your deliberations." (Emphasis added)

(The jury again retired from the courtroom).

Defendant, after the jury retired, made the following objection :

"Your Honor, there is one exception we want to note, the defendant conceives that one of the elements involved in the jury arriving at a unanimous verdict, that it is not a proper element to consider time consumed in the trial or the expenses of the Government and the taxpayers, of which the jury is a member, we think that is an improper consideration, and that those things of time and expense are immaterial so long as a just verdict is arrived at, *we think the Court should not have instructed the jury on the matter of the amount of taxes and expense which would be involved and particularly applying it to the jury as taxpayers*, we think that that might be calculated either one way or the other to make the jury feel like that it is their duty to cut the time down.

THE COURT OVERRULED THE EXCEPTION.

While the jury was out the second time, Judge Thomason told John Cofer that, in his opinion, Daddy had won the trial. I don't know if he intended his remark to be ironic. While we were waiting for the verdict, Jan and I slept on benches in the Federal Building,

RESIDENT
yndon B. Johnson

To Billie Sol Estes
with warm regards and best wishes
Lyndon B. Johnson

SPEAKER OF THE HOUSE
Samuel Rayburn

For Billy Sol Estes
with good wishes of
Sam Rayburn
1961

ENATOR
alph Yarborough

To A Great Friend, True Texan,
Great American – Billie Sol Estes of Pecos;
With warmest appreciation
Ralph W. Yarborough
Washington, D.C. 1958.

ABOVE/Daddy appears in the role he loved best — Political Kingmaker. Nex Daddy is Congressman George Mahon head of Appropriations and in center F Maston who at his death recently gave Abilene Christian University their large donation in history.

AT LEFT/Daddy sent 200 black stude to school per year in his hey day. Pictu with him are (top right) Arthur Fulson, now a missionary in Africa, (below left Jimmy Brown, now a gospel preacher, (right) Floyd Rose, who is now one of heads of NAACP and a well known educator.

MIDDLE FAR RIGHT/Frank Cleme the Governor of Tennessee, and Dad became fast friends and business associates after they were selected to t Outstanding Young Men of the Unite States together.

ABOVE/Dressed in mink for the Inaugural Ball, Mother and Daddy posed with Mr. and Mrs. Clyde Marshall, (center). He was President of Commercial Solvents, who financed all the tanks. At right is A.B. Foster and his wife. He handled all Daddy's paperwork, but escaped criminal problems.

LEFT/In 1960, Daddy and Mother are pictured with Senator and Mrs. Ralph Yarborough. Daddy made huge contributions to his election. Smiling Ralph was to later say, "Billie Sol who?"

WIDE WORLD PHOTOS

WIDE WORLD PHOTOS

AT LEFT/In El Paso, Daddy was sentenced to 15 years in prison. Pictured are Daddy, and his two brothers, John L Jr., to the right of Daddy, and Word bo tom left, and their Uncle Sol B. Estes, who had just renewed his bail.

TOP LEFT/This conviction was later overturned in the appeals court. At far le is Finis Mothershead, AP reporter who befriended us.

AT RIGHT/1962 — Daddy and John Cofer at Tyler, Texas trial. We had our future in his hands.

WIDE WORLD PHOTOS

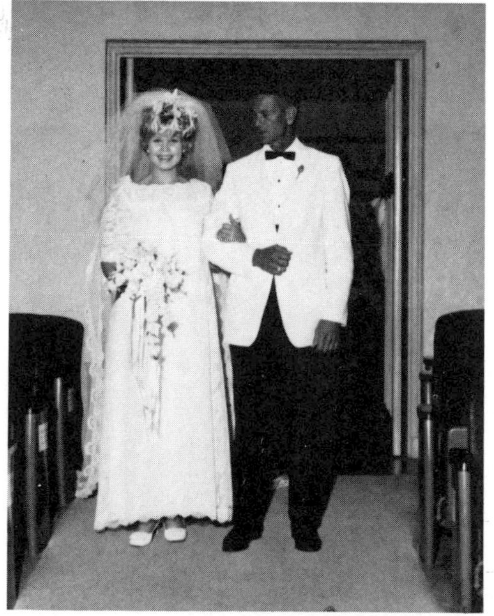

TOP PHOTO/Found Guilty — Daddy with Mother on his arm walk from the Federal Court Building in El Paso. Behind them are Uncle John with his wife.

BOTTOM LEFT/In May of 1969, my Uncle Dr. John L. Estes walked me down the aisle at my wedding. He was always there when I needed him.

TOP RIGHT/Daddy and Mother and sister Dawn leave the La Tuna Federal Correction institution at midnight following his parole. In front seat is sister, Joy and brother Billie Jr. is driving.

BOTTOM RIGHT/In July, 1971, just days after Daddy was released from prison, we celebrated Mother and Daddy's 25th wedding anniversary. The looked so confident of the future.

DE WORLD PHOTOS

UNITED PRESS INTERNATIONAL

WIDE WORLD PHOTOS

WIDE WORLD PHOTOS

HELLY KATZ/PEOPLE WEEKLY/ c 1983 TIME INC.

SHELLY KATZ/PEOPLE WEEKLY/ c 1983 TIME INC.

OSITE PAGE TOP PHOTO/
her collapsed on the hot Dallas street
wing Daddy's conviction and my
r Dawn's husband, Danny Stevens,
ed Mother back to the hotel.

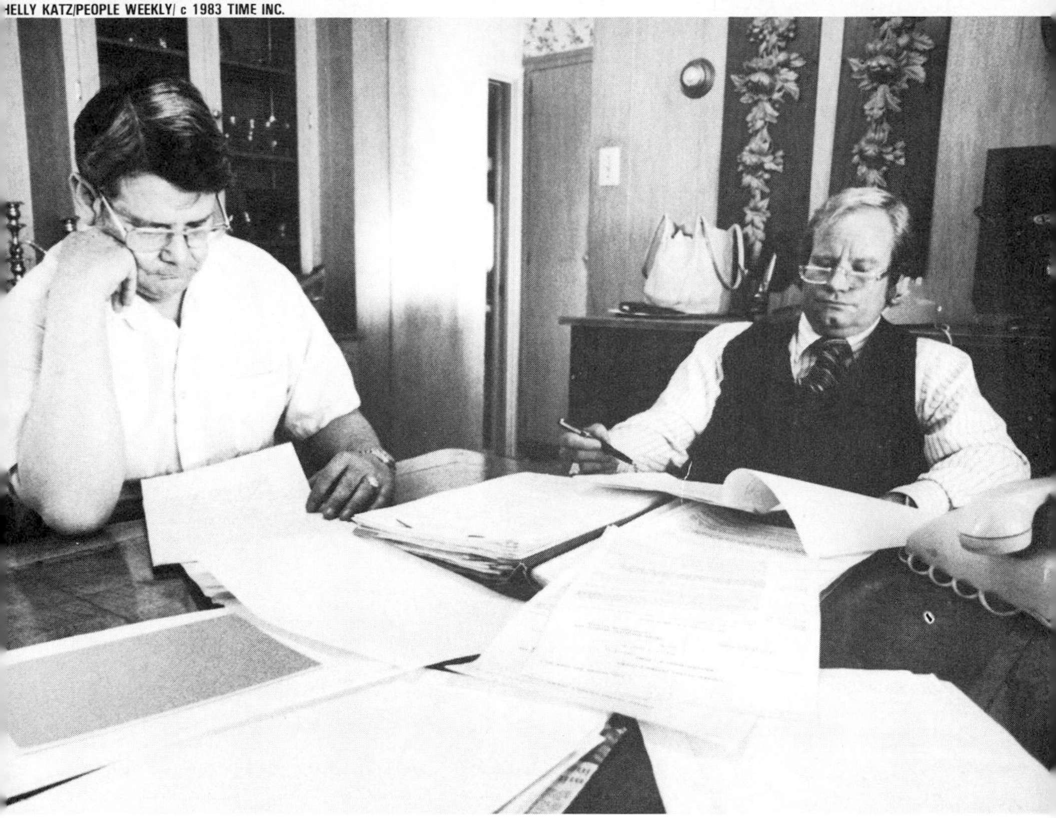

DLE PHOTO/Daddy had just been
icted again. Just behind Daddy on his
s my sister, Dawn and to her right was
usband, Walter. Daddy's lawyer,
Irwin's hand can be seen holding
dy's left arm.

TOM PHOTO/Daddy, left, and
her, center, leave federal court after he
sentenced to 10 years in prison.

PHOTO/During the plea bargain
tiations, Daddy and his attorney,
Irwin, struggle through mounds of
r work on Mother and Daddy's din-
oom table.

RIGHT/Daddy, wearing the Rolex
h his employees had given him in the
was fighting the Government in the
to remain a free man.

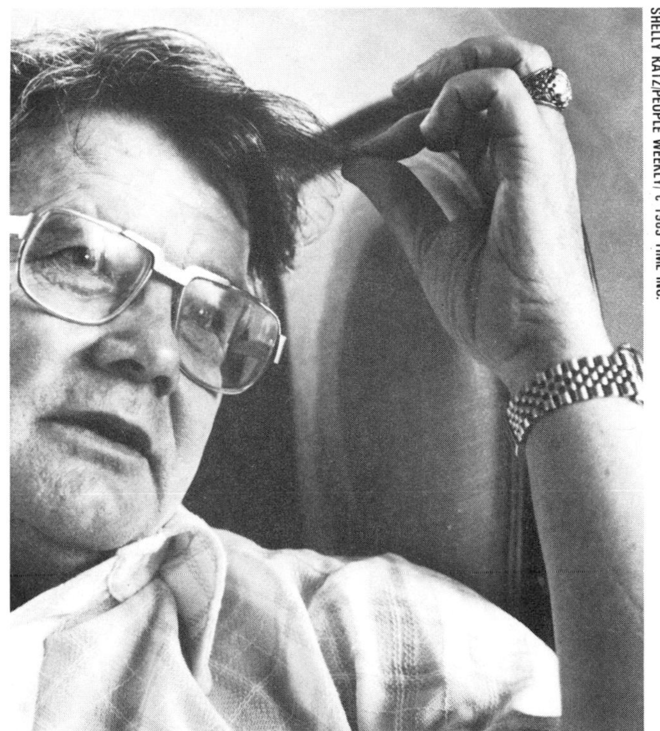

ABOVE/We met Willie Nelson in front of the Big Spring Prison Camp. Pictured are L-R Billie Jr., Pam, Willie, Jan, Walter, and Sue Goolsby (kneeling).

RIGHT/In this picture, taken by People Magazine, they said, "Billie Sol is up a creek, but never without a paddle."

and Dawn, Billie and Joy played in the halls. We all stayed at the old Cortez Hotel facing the town plaza, once the grandest between Dallas and Los Angeles. There was a fountain in the plaza with alligators that were nearly 100 years old. They were brought there as babies and had been amusing tourists ever since. It was there that my little grandmother, MaMa, after the verdict was announced, hit one of the photographers with her purse and made national news. It was the last trial she ever attended.

When the jury came back with a guilty verdict, which was inevitable after the judge's dynamite charge, Daddy was sentenced to 15 years. I will never forget the bleak feeling we all shared. We were broke, exhausted, emotionally spent and seemingly friendless. On the day we were leaving El Paso for good, I remember watching as Mr. and Mrs. Cofer set out for a vacation trip to Mexico—on the last of our money.

VIII CHAPTER

Exodus from the Desert

One night in the summer of 1963, I went with a friend to the drive-in picture show in Pecos. As we sat there watching the movie, I suddenly had a premonition that I should go home right away. I told my date and we left. As we pulled into the driveway, we heard a gunshot. I ran into the house and turned on the lights in the living room. Daddy shouted, "Turn off those lights and get on the floor." We called the police, and when they came we found a bullet lodged in the safety plate-glass windows of the living room.

The phone had rung. Daddy's brother Bob had said, "Billie, let me get it." When he answered the phone, the bullet was fired and the phone went dead. A policeman measured the place where the bullet hit the glass—right on target for Daddy's or Bob's stomach.

The police investigated, but they were unable to find a suspect. After a few questions were asked, the case seemed to be forgotten.

Shortly after the shot was fired at the living room window, Mother and Daddy quietly made the decision that we would leave our home of 10 years.

Although Daddy had secret hopes that he would remain free, he knew then that it was just a matter of a few weeks until he would go to prison, and he wanted us to be in Abilene near his brother and his parents, who lived in Clyde. Also, it had become a very real possibility that if we stayed in Pecos he would be killed. The police there had been unable or unwilling to solve the mystery of who fired the shot at the window. We couldn't be sure that we would be safer in Abilene, but at least, we would feel less vulnerable.

To me, leaving our home in Pecos is still the most shattering experience of my life. Even now, 20 years later, it's hard for me to think about it without becoming physically sick. It seemed then that we were giving up our only secure refuge just when we needed it most.

Mother didn't discuss the move with us. She just had a bunch of large boxes delivered and informed us that we were going to Abilene to stay with Uncle John L. and Aunt June until things calmed down. She did not say that we would never come back. She gave each of us three boxes, told us to go to our rooms and pack everything that we wanted to take. I went upstairs and started packing. Mother came up later and said, "Don't fuss, just throw your stuff in the boxes because we're leaving today." So, I took all of my stuffed animals and sweaters and didn't even have time to call up my friends to tell them I was leaving.

While we were loading the car, photographers and news reporters came at us from all directions. Suddenly, they were everywhere, on the lawn, in the driveway, and near the car. That was one of the rare times my mother lost her temper. One woman reporter had been rudely persistent, trying to get us to make statements. We were all still depressed and shocked and didn't need any further harassment, so Mother impatiently chased her off the property.

We finished loading the car quickly and drove away from Pecos. Mother and Daddy were crying. We children, with our pets on our arms, were crying. We were in our white Cadillac because our limousine and my convertible had already been confiscated. The bankruptcy laws at that time permitted us to keep one car.

We drove all night until we arrived at Uncle John L.'s home. They tried to make us feel welcome, but this being the most miserable experience of my 13 years, it was impossible for me to be happy. All of our belongings were placed in storage and Mother and Daddy began looking at houses. At that time, there were many houses on the market in Abilene, so after a long search Mother and Daddy finally narrowed their choices down to two.

We stayed with Uncle John L. and Aunt June for a number of weeks. Then, in the middle of the night before the first day of school, the movers arrived with all of our belongings and dumped them at our new home, 70 Castle Drive. We moved in right away but had to sleep on the floor that first night. The next morning we got up and searched through the mounds of boxes for our clothes, got dressed and started out for our first day of school in Abilene. When we went outside that morning there were news reporters hiding in the bushes, just like in Pecos, but we quickly eluded them.

That day, I started the 10th grade at Cooper High School, a very large school where one class had more students in it than the whole school in Pecos. I did not have a single friend. I knew no one and I was frightened.

The year before, I had been elected the class favorite and was an officer in my class. I made a personal vow that I was going to be happy going to school in Abilene, and that I was going to be accepted.

I had worried about how people were going to react to me. We had all been on TV and in the newspapers, and when I got to school, all these kids knew who I was but I didn't know any of them.

Abilene seemed to me to be very different from Pecos. There were several small cliques of Junior League-type girls at Cooper High that excluded me. That bothered me for a while because I was always used to being the daughter of the richest man in town.

Dawn became a member of the school band. She wanted to play the saxophone but seemed to have a problem keeping track of it. One day as she was getting out of Mother's station wagon, she put the saxophone down in front of the car and Mother ran over it. That ended her band career.

My brother Billie was the most unhappy about the move from Pecos to Abilene. It took him a number of years to adjust. But, by the time he was a senior at Cooper High School, he was president of his class.

One of the first clues that our lifestyle was going to be different after our move to Abilene came at our first dinner at Aunt June's. In Pecos, we never knew who or how many people Daddy was going to bring home to dinner, so there was always lots of extra food prepared to accommodate the extra guests. We sometimes had guests for breakfast, some who had spent the night and some who hadn't. Sometimes Daddy would, if he saw someone who looked hungry, impulsively bring them to dinner. It had been well known around Pecos that if you were hungry at about six o'clock in the evening and didn't have anyplace to eat, you would be welcome at the Estes household.

Aunt June's house was run a little differently. She had been a home economics major at Abilene Christian University, and she knew, to a bite, the amount of food each person required for optimum health, and that is what she served. I don't mean to imply that she was stingy—no one who had just taken seven relatives into her home could be suspected of that. But we had never been around such a high degree of efficiency and frugality, and none of us kids knew what to make of it. That first dinner consisted of a delicious casserole and sliced tomatoes that exactly served 10 people. There wasn't going to be any more, and, to a child who had once won an eating contest with an adult, that was a real shock.

DADDY NEVER ACCEPTED THE REALITY that he was going to jail. Lyndon had promised him that he wouldn't, and Daddy was still trusting in Lyndon. Mother, I think, was more realistic and had been preparing herself for the inevitable. I was a believer, along with Daddy, in Lyndon. Daddy was living his life firmly with that belief, going about the business of salvaging as much of our lives as he could and trying to minimize the impact of the bankruptcy.

One winter evening in 1964, about a year after we had moved into our new home, the marshals rang the bell at 70 Castle Drive and asked to see Daddy. They were shown into the kitchen where Daddy was helping prepare supper. One of the marshals said, "Mr Estes, we have to inform you that you are under arrest." They were polite, as usual, and Daddy went with them quietly and cooperatively, also as usual.

I had to watch them handcuff Daddy and take him away. I didn't have time to prepare myself for it, so my feeling was of numbing shock. We were still, at that point, so emotionally dependent on Daddy that I instantly felt lost. However, Mother was determined that we were not going to fall apart, so I had to go to my room and finish my homework as if nothing had happend.

Being my Daddy's daughter, as soon as the shock wore off, I returned to optimism. Neither Daddy nor I believed that he would stay in jail long; that Lyndon would keep his promise and get him set free. But, by that time LBJ had become President and the stakes had changed. Daddy was no longer any real use to him, and LBJ had become much more vulnerable. While vice president, he, like all vice presidents, had been universally ignored by both press and politicians. Now that he was President he couldn't show his surgical scar or yank his dogs by the ears without provoking instant and far reaching press hysteria. How was he going to arrange a Presidential pardon for Daddy without inciting a full scale riot in the press room at the White House? As the months wore on, that reality began to sink in, and we began to realize that Daddy was going to be in jail for a long time.

THE MARSHALS TOOK DADDY BY CAR to Leavenworth, a trip which took two and a half days. At night, they housed him in small town jails. He said he had nothing to eat during the whole trip from Abilene to Leavenworth, Ka. Once, in one of the jails on the way he was offered what he described as a "green piece of Bologna." He added, "The other men in the jail wanted to fight over it, so I just let them have it."

I KNEW WHAT VISITING DADDY AT Leavenworth was going to be like because I had seen all the old prison movies. Guns were mounted on the prison's outside walls. It looked bleak and menacing, but we were able to visit in a real visiting room rather than through bars or a glass window. We were allowed no physical contact with Daddy because of the possibility of smuggling drugs and weapons. Considering the number of weapons and amounts of drugs floating around Leavenworth, that appears to have been a wasted security effort.

The other inmates I saw on my first visit looked like what I supposed were typical gangster types, and that is what they were. Leavenworth was a place for murderers doing life sentences and big time gangsters. Daddy's prisonmates had names you would recognize, such as Vito Genevese, the Godfather of the Mafia. Daddy was put into "D" section, the place for the worst criminals in the United States. Daddy's number there was 6624.

Since many of the prisoners were there for life with nothing to lose, killing another inmate was part of a day's fun. Daddy was an excellent potential target for some of these men because he had had so much publicity, and by the time he got to Leavenworth, his name was a household word. Therefore, he had a big name, and anybody who killed him would gain status and become something of a big name himself.

One day while Daddy was in the recreation area watching a gocart race, one of the racers ran him down and severely injured his back. The word was out that Daddy would make a prime target for assassination, and the race was on to see who would win the trophy.

Uncle John L. tells the story like this. "Because Mr. Cofer (in examining a witness at Daddy's trial) called the inmates of Leavenworth murderers, peons, and sex perverts, word had gone out at Leavenworth to 'get Billie Sol' in retaliation for his attorney's remarks. Billie Sol got the word one day while getting his hair cut by an inmate. When he heard the story, he asked the barber, 'aren't you getting out soon?' and the man replied, 'As a matter of fact, I'm being paroled tomorrow.'

"Would you get in touch with my brother when you get out so he can try to get me moved?'

"So the inmate showed up at my office very soon after he was released—it might even have been the next day. He got to the office about 4 o'clock in the afternoon. I had about 15 patients backed up, so I asked him if he could wait. By this time it was not unusual to have people showing up at my office going on about Bill—some were ex-prisoners, some had schemes. I had long ago learned how to weed them out. So he told his story and he told it very vividly. He named names, told where he had heard it, told why, and warned me that it would happen soon in the future.

"Well, I had had enough experience with ex-prison inmates coming around for money that I didn't believe him, so I said, 'Mister, I'm going to call your hand on this.' So I reached over my desk and picked up the phone and called the prison. The warden had already gone home so I called him there and repeated the story I had just heard.

"The warden thanked me for calling and promised that he would put his ear to the ground and find out if Bill really was in danger. The next day he called me. Without telling me how he found out, he confirmed that the threat was true. 'We took him right out of the exercise yard,' he said, 'We didn't even let him go back to his cell to get his toothbrush. He's right now on his way to a prison in Sandstone, Minnesota.'

"The end of the story is that the ex-con who brought me this story wanted money. At that time we just didn't have any money, so I would give him the day's cash receipts. He came about once a week for several weeks, then he went to Las Vegas. He called collect from there several times, but I never would take the calls. I heard later that he got killed there."

Daddy spent several weeks in the prison hospital recovering from attack. The man in the next bed was Vito Genevese. Daddy said to me recently, "He was the kindest man I ever met. He had a bad heart and loved his family, but he never spoke of the Mafia." He told Daddy frequently, "Billie, keep your big mouth shut if you like breathing."

Daddy recalls, "One night we had china on the table and were eating steaks. Both were contraband. A young guard came in and said he was going to tell his superior. He did and the superior replied, 'You can report them if you want, but leave me out of it.' " The Mafia ruled Leavenworth and Daddy's friendship with Genevese helped him survive. He said he was comfortable and safe with him. The guards didn't mess with any of the Mafia guys.

At Sandstone, a medium security prison, Daddy found inmates he could better identify with. They were businessmen, doctors, lawyers, mayors, city council members, and other white collar criminals. Daddy made some close friends there who helped make his time there more bearable.

He converted one of his Sandstone guards, Howard Osgood. One night in his cell, Daddy was reading his Bible when he looked out and saw Mr. Osgood. He asked him what was the matter and the guard said, "In my own way I am also a prisoner here." Daddy talked to him about Christ and how Christianity could give him a whole new life. Daddy enrolled him in a Bible course through the College Church of Christ in Abilene, and Mr. Osgood later became a Christian. He and his wife had a daughter, and they named her Joy, after my youngest sister.

ON MARCH 27, 1970, DADDY WAS transferred from Sandstone to La Tuna. La Tuna is located on a mountain about 20 miles outside of El Paso in Anthony, Texas. The prison entrance is on a road which goes up the hill through prison farmland. There is a tall watch tower with a guard in it. The prison is white stucco and resembles a Mexican fortress with black iron bars on the windows. There are no guns mounted on the walls, as at Leavenworth, because it is a medium security prison.

After entering the parking lot, visitors stop at a loud speaker intercom. "Why are you here?" the guard asks. "State your business. Do you have a gun?" After passing through the front door of the complex, we stopped at a table where a guard was seated. He would carefully check Daddy's card to see if each of us was on the visiting list, then he would make certain that no more than four at a time went in to visit. This made it difficult for us because we had a large family. Several of us would remain in the car or in front of the prison while four visited with Daddy.

After checking in, we walked through a gate which was opened by pressing a button. After we were locked in a holding pen, another door unlocked to allow us to go inside the visiting room. In warm weather, there was more room because we could sit outside on benches in an enclosed courtyard. There were also picnic tables in front of the prison, and Daddy was permitted to sit with us there because he was a jail trusty.

Lunches could be bought there for 60 cents each. We are not very particular about food, but I must admit their lunches were the worst I have ever eaten. Daddy never complained about them, and we tried to act like we weren't hungry, or that we just wanted candy and coke from the vending machines.

At La Tuna, Daddy was librarian, and he took care of the officer's clubhouse and swimming pool. Since many of the Mexican inmates could not read, his job as librarian was not very demanding. He enjoyed his other job because to get outside of the prison walls and into the clubhouse was a treat—even as a janitor.

Daddy continued his routine of self-discipline at La Tuna, which had begun at Leavenworth AA meetings. He was very active in the Gaval Club and attended religious services. Daddy converted several Mexican prisoners, and some of them are now ministers in Mexico.

Daddy started drinking while in jail, and Alcoholics Anonymous became very important in his life. AA is actually a religion. The 12 steps of AA very closely resemble the principles of Christianity. Also for Daddy, the traditional chapel services at prison had little resemblence to the Church of Christ. The personal involvement that AA members have with the organizations and with each other was important to them all. Another reason that AA is very important in prisons is because it helps redirect aggressions away from violence and helps make the inevitable tensions of prison life more bearable.

While Daddy was home on a furlough, he became very upset over a minor incident, so instead of getting drunk, overeating, or becoming hostile, as some people might do, or as Daddy himself might have done before joining AA, he asked Mother to drop him off at an AA meeting in Abilene. When she picked him up two hours later, he was very calm and controlled, having worked through the problem with fellow AA members.

Daddy says more than 90 per cent of the people in prison would not be there if they had not had an alcohol-related problem at the time they committed their crimes. Unfortunately, prison promotes alcoholism. Daddy became an alcoholic shortly after he got to Leavenworth. There, the alcohol was kept in the fire extinguishers and Daddy was in charge of checking them and keeping them charged—charged with liquor. "Alcohol," he said, "flows very freely there, as at all prisons."

It's ironic that the one thing that sent Daddy to jail the second time, the recordings that the undercover cops had made, would have sounded innocent and nonincriminating if Daddy had not been drinking at the time they were made. When they were played for the jury, Daddy's slurred speech and abusive language counteracted all the sympathy the jury had developed for him.

IT'S VERY HARD FOR PRISONERS TO write letters because they are so heavily censored. That means most letters from prison are on very general terms and can never reveal what really goes on there. Nevertheless, Daddy's letters are important to us because, except for our occasional visits, they were the only communication we could have with him. They were always filled with expressions of love and sometimes one of his famous pithy aphorisms such as "Multiply by dividing."

The following are some of the many letters we got from Daddy while he was in prison:

August 3, 1969

My Precious Children

"Human nature has not changed since the beginning of man. You have hate, and love.

The key is the control of man. If you can control the emotions of man, you can control him. You can block profanity out of your mind. You just don't know. You have a conscious mind and a self-conscious mind."

Life is mathematics. Every Wednesday we have a class at the chapel classroom. A man is talking about speed-reading. He said his daughters took speed-reading in college. A guy is talking about the beauty in writing. He said if you read too fast he would miss some of its beauty.

(A proverb is a short sentence based on a lot of experience.)

August 12, 1969

Dearest Walter and Pamie,

Today is a cloudy, warm Tuesday here. I can't keep from thinking about the cold weather we have had. Old Jack Frost will arrive here this month probably, and it will leave behind some beautiful leaves on this wooded land. It will leave the corn crop that didn't have time to mature. We will have about 60 days of beautiful fall weather. Indian Summer. The most beautiful sunsets, and the weather will be just right. An outdoor air-conditioning system to control it couldn't do as well. So, September and October we have beautiful weather here. Weather you would really like. I saw a mother deer, and her little live deer last Sunday. Something so beautiful to see. A mother deer and her two little ones. They watched her and she lead the way for them to come out and graze. She seemed to say, "All is well, nothing will hurt you, come on out and get some exercise, and some good green grass." I couldn't keep from thinking too, that soon the snow will fill the air, and the ground will be covered. Then food won't be so plentiful. Last winter was sure a bad winter for the deer. Many did not survive the winter, due to a shortage of food. The snow was so deep on the ground the deer couldn't run fast enough to get away from the dogs and wolves. So they would be caught and killed. On television I saw a great act of kindness. Some people were feeding the deer. A lot of people fed the deer. They would have a grader grade off a strip, and put food in it for the deer. We have some black bear here. The black bear, I understand, you can hunt them all year around.

We have a pair of robins, after spending the summer in the south, come back here and they have some baby robins. I enjoy watching them feed their babies. I love you both more each day. I think about you both. I pray for you both. You are both so precious to me. With so much love and so proud of you both.
Dad

•

August 22, 1969

Precious Children,

I am at an A.A. meeting we had an interesting speaker. A medical Doctor who is 95 years old. He was in prison here. He makes a real good talk.

(He said society, when we left prison, wouldn't put their arms around us, but we could put our arms around them, and they would accept us.)
He said he was talking from experience.

•

June 27, 1970

My Dearest Walter and Pamie,

I have been thinking a lot about Don and Jan's wedding, like same as I did about your wedding.

So many things have happened since I went away, haven't they. Pamie to Cooper, graduation, to college, graduation, then your marriage. I hope that it all work out. When you got married I said a prayer for you, and meditated while the wedding was going on. I am doing the same at Don and Jan's wedding.

I am so very proud of you all, and I love you all so very much. More each day. My thoughts are always with you both. I pray for you both all the time. I miss you both so very much.

I will close for now.
All my love to each
Dad

•

Dearest Children,

To day is Monday. Sure hope you both have a most wonderful day. I love you both so very much. You are both so precious. The trouble in Attica, New York is the harvest of many hard ships imposed on the Prisoners, for a long period of time. A lack of communication between the officers and the men. The officers as a whole are not qualified to be over the men. The worse qualification is they don't have love for the inmates. Hate breeds hate. Love would breed love. The men are going to have to be taught to love and not to hate. Taught to have faith in mankind. Then they will give love instead of hate. Hate just built up to a point that it could not be controlled. Christianity, its teachings are the only answer to the prisons. They have tried many other things, maybe some they will try Christian principles in the prisons. Non-Christian guards cannot apply Christian principles. I hope some day they will have prisons run in a Christian way. Christ's teachings can't be improved up on. Man's way will fail in the prison

reform as they always have. . .
All my love,
Dad

ALMOST TWO YEARS AFTER DADDY LEFT for prison, on June 6, 1966, I started summer school at Abilene Christian University, the day after I graduated from high school. It was assumed from the time I was in elementary school that I would go to ACU. Of course, back then, it was also assumed that when I went to college, I would have my own apartment and my lilac Cadillac, and I would be indulged in the manner to which I had become accustomed. When the time came to start college, the reality was quite a bit different. Uncle John L. told me that if I took a half-time job and went to school half-time, he would help me through. That and a $200 per semester tuition scholarship got me through college.

By that time I had ceased being the spoiled, overindulged rich brat who petulantly threw unwanted parts of her hamburger out of the limousine window at a drive-in restaraunt and had gotten serious about herself and her future.

My first job at ACU was in the public relations department. It was to prepare press releases about students who had won awards, athletic events, or done anything positive or attention-getting and to send the releases to hometown newspapers. The job paid 60 cents an hour. I was not paid in cash, but the earnings were deducted from my tuition bill, so I never saw any of my wages.

I decided to get my degree in journalism and work in communications. I started working on the student newspaper and began making lots of good friends. Living in the dormitory instead of at home also helped me make friends. By my second year I was news editor of the paper. In my third and final year in college

(I finished in three years), I became editor of the paper, and that paid my full tuition. I also spent one semester at Temple University in Philadelphia, taking some special journalism classes. To pay for that, I saved money I had earned from babysitting.

I met my husband, Walter Tedford, in 1968, my second year in college. I actually met him twice. In my first year, he sat next to me in Chapel, but he smelled of cigarette smoke so I went to the dean and had my seat changed. The next year, he turned up sitting next to me in class, and by the following spring, we were engaged.

The day we finished our finals in our senior year, we got married. We decided we wanted to move to Hawaii so Walter's parents, for a wedding gift, gave us $10,000 plus a honeymoon trip to Hawaii. We drove our car out through New Mexico and Arizona, stopping at the Grand Canyon where I had my first alcoholic drink, then Las Vegas, Disney Land, and finally San Francisco. We checked our car onto a freighter, embarked on the cruiseship, *Lurlene*, and sailed to Honolulu. We were the youngest people aboard ship and took a good bit of teasing about being newlyweds. We also took a good bit of champagne, which I had never tasted, not even at my wedding.

After three months of job hunting Walter got homesick. Jobs for recent graduates in Hawaii were almost nonexistent since many other young people also moved to Hawaii. So we moved to Wichita Falls, Texas where Walter had planned to work for his father's company. However when we got there, Walter's parents were off touring Europe. He decided he wanted another degree and we returned to Abilene where Walter re-enrolled in school and I went to work at an advertising agency as the media director and complaint department for the *Herald of Truth*, a Church of Christ sponsored television and film series.

The next year we moved to Houston where I went to work for a real estate developer and Walter finally got to go to work for his father's company as a sales representative. The name of the company was Foster Cathead Company and had been founded by Walter's grandfather who invented the cat-head tool, which takes apart the draw works on an oil rig. He became a multimillionaire and his company had offices all over the world.

In November 1970, about six months before Daddy was to be paroled, we returned to Abilene from Houston for the ACU homecoming. Our family was well and for once everything seemed calm and serene. Dawn had a part in a student musical. Billie and Joy were happy and in school.

However, beneath this sea of tranquility was the usual turbulence. The government had filed a suit against Mother, Uncle John L. and Uncle Word for mishandling our trust fund—settled in our favor sometime later. The government had a lien against us for back taxes. Since the government can take any personal belongings for income tax owed, and since, according to the IRS, Daddy owed in the neighborhood of some $22 million dollars, we all expected government agents to drive up any day and start taking our furniture and personal possessions. Mother says Daddy told her to hide her wedding ring, but she could not bear to take it off. She still has it.

IX CHAPTER

Daddy's Home Again

The following is an excerpt from my diary entry of April 14, 1971:

Daddy should go before the Parole Board this week or maybe next. We are supposed to have an answer by the end of April. We are trying not to get too excited and have our hopes dashed like we did last year. When he was turned down we were all sick with disappointment. He has been a model prisoner with good behavior, but I don't believe that makes very much difference. MaMa and Papa John were at La Tuna a few weeks ago, and as they were leaving the chaplain told them not to get their hopes too high.

I think our family has been too quiet. I believe if we picketed the White House and used tougher tactics we might get somewhere. We have tried to avoid publicity, but now it seems we would have been better off if we had caused a scene. John L. says if we get a "no" he will go on national television and demand to know why.

We don't understand why robbers and murderers are paroled but Daddy is not. His spirits are still high and he is hopeful.

Jimmy Hoffa was turned down a couple of weeks ago on his second time to go before the Board. However, he was allowed a five-day leave because his wife is very ill. He is allowed to call her every evening. Daddy was very sad when he disappeared. They shared a mutual dislike . . . Robert Kennedy. . . .

April 27, 1971, the day the decision of the Parole Board was to be announced, the Associated Press ran a story by Clayton Hickerson: "A decade ago, the chubby fertilizer entrepreneur was the shining example held up to members of the 4-H Clubs of America. He was a Church of Christ lay preacher. He was the darling of the Junior Chamber of Commerce. Anywhere in the United States, he was known as a financial genius, a boy wonder. In short, he was 'Mr. Big.' "

Allis Sanders, "The Motorman," wrote in his column in the *Houston Chronicle* on May 3, 1971, "We all know that BSE lived lavishly before Uncle Fuzz dropped on him. (When you are selling millions of dollars worth of non-existent fertilizer tanks, you can afford to live lavishly.)" Sanders quoted from a story printed the previous week in Houston: "He had three tennis courts, two airplanes and a Cadillac in the driveway. With a driveway like that, think what the rest of the home must have been like."

This is just an example of some of the reporting that was to await Daddy upon his return from prison.

Betty Hughes, *Abilene Reporter-News* women's editor, wrote an accurate story telling of the parole. Mrs. Hughes also wrote an excellent, factual story in 1970 when Daddy's first bid for parole was turned down. Mrs. Hughes is the only reporter to whom Mother gave an interview.

The Associated Press ran a story one newspaper headlined "Many Residents of Pecos Would Welcome Estes." We are happy to see a favorable article. The reporter was not given a by-line, but I am thankful to him or her for writing an unmalicious story. It was not completely without negative comments, but if it had been, it would have lost its reality. Among those who commented that they would be happy to see Daddy back in Pecos was Joe Stafford, a member of the church our family attended (his wife was Daddy's secretary for years). The story went on to say, "Ray McPherson, a former banker, said 'much of the town was, and is, sympathetic. They seem to feel he was paying the price for others besides himself.' Orb Rowden, a managing editor of the *Pecos Enterprise,* said, 'Estes had helped many people get into business and his conviction hurt those people.' Bill Hubbs, owner of Pecos radio station KIUM, said he was pleased to see the parole. Daddy's youngest brother, Word, said, 'The family already has received too much publicity, and I would prefer not to comment."

ON APRIL 27, 1971 THE U.S. PAROLE BOARD in Washington announced that Daddy would be paroled July 12. Mother, Uncle John L. and Aunt June had gone to Washington to ask again for parole. They went before the board in January, 1970, but were turned down. The Parole Board set December, 1971, as the next possible hearing for parole. Fred Bonavita, Washington bureau reporter for the *Houston Post* wrote; "George J. Reed, Parole Board chairman, agreed to the advanced hearing. Estes, whose first request for parole was denied in January, 1970, was not to have been heard again until next December. Mr. Estes' lawyers made a request for the earlier review and the board reviewed the request and advanced the date," Reed wrote. "There was considerable data presented when the request for review was made," he wrote.

Although his parole made headlines across the country, most people probably just read it and forgot about it. But for my family and close friends, it was not a headline to be forgotten. This was one of the first promising and optimistic occurrences in 10 years of uncertainty and bad headlines.

I was very tense. I went to work that day with a headache and a feeling of nausea. I turned on a radio at my desk and waited anxiously for the news each hour.

At about 3 p.m., Mother called collect from Washington. I asked the operator to charge it to my home phone and waited impatiently for Mother to give me the Parole Board's decision.

Mother said, "Pam . . . Then she started crying. I knew then that he had lost his bid for parole a second time. I said, "Mother, he didn't make it?" She sobbed and finally said, "No, he *did* get it; he is going to come home to us." I cried, then we laughed, and Mother just kept repeating, "They are going to let him come home." I asked her when, and she said July 12. I said, "Why July 12?" She said, "I don't know why, I'm just glad." He'd be home for their 25th wedding anniversary which was July 14.

I WAS SO EXCITED AND HAPPY I COULD hardly contain myself, but I picked up the phone and called other family members.

About 3:30 p.m. the news was released to the press, and Twila Duncan, a close friend from ACU, called to say how happy she was. She said she had thought about it all day and was so happy for us.

The *Abilene Reporter-News* had called before I got home wanting to know where Mother was staying in Washington, but we didn't know. Mr. Woodworth, my boss, let me go home early from work because he knew I was bubbling with excitement and wouldn't be any help at the office. Walter and I went out to dinner to celebrate with another couple, and when we got home the *Abilene Reporter-News* called again. I told them I still didn't know where Mother was staying, but we were very happy about the parole and we were looking forward to having Daddy home.

Pat Batts, a college classmate in radio-television, called to tape an interview for a Waco station where he was assistant news director. He was a little hesitant to ask for our comments, but I know what it's like to need an interview so I happily cooperated.

Many other people called to wish us well. It was one of those times when we felt we had the support of the whole world, a rare treat for us.

Daddy was released from La Tuna Prison at 12:03 a.m., Monday, July 12, 1971. Mother, Dawn, Billie and Joy drove to El Paso to pick him up. Daddy served six years, four months and one week in prison. Billie drove and Joy sat in the front seat with him. Mother and Dawn, sat on either side of Daddy in the back. Several reporters waited at the entrance gate and followed them into El Paso, trying to get a picture for their newspaper and television audiences.

Billic drove to a small motel where we had often stayed when visiting Daddy. After celebrating on a feast of steak, Daddy spent his first night outside of prison walls in 6½ years. Tuesday, they drove to Abilene. Daddy was so thrilled to be home again. Mother says he seemed to be in a daze, walking from room to room to find our home to be the same as he had remembered it. Mother says at first he was almost hysterical with happiness, and he felt as if it were just a good dream, and that any minute he would awaken and be back in prison.

Daddy had so much fun telling of his experiences in jail. He told everyone "how great it is to be out of jail." He enjoyed his clean shower, good-smelling soap, soft towels and clean sheets. He loved the freedom of walking out of doors and moments of privacy. He was constantly on the phone or greeting guests at the door. He was so anxious to talk to all his friends, shake their hands and hear their voices.

We planned a combination "Welcome Home" and 25th wedding anniversary party for Mother and Daddy.

Mail poured in (about 100 letters a day). The door bell rang and both telephone lines rang constantly. On Friday the florist trucks began arriving with potted plants and flowers from friends from Abilene and all across the country. Old friends from Clyde, new friends and Daddy's chaplain from El Paso sent flowers. A local florist sent Mother and Daddy complimentary flowers. Old Pecos friends sent gifts and cards. We sent out 300 invitations, asking people to come between 7 and 9 p.m. Daddy wrote about 250 personal letters from prison asking them to come from 5 to 7 p.m. He was confused about the time, but it worked out well because it divided up the hundreds of people who attended. Guests began arriving at four o'clock and the last guests left at about 11 p.m. Some 500 guests signed the guest book, but we felt there were several hundred more than that. And the dishwashers, our cousins, agreed.

We were thrilled and surprised by the huge turnout. By 5:30 p.m. we ran out of lemonade and gingerale for the punch, and we had to make two trips to the store for more. And the party wasn't actually supposed to start until seven o'clock.

The women guests came dressed in everything from formal dresses to pant suits. My sister Dawn wore orange velour hot pants. Daddy loved his new suit which my brother Billie bought him. The clothes he loved to wear 10 years before were finally in style. The white shoes and wide ties which were considered ostentacious in

1961 were perfect in 1971.

Daddy's readjustment to everyday life after seven years in prison was both difficult and humorous. After being locked up for several years, instant freedom was difficult, and readjustment was gradual. Such simple things as showering, eating meals and driving the car were a real challenge to him the first few days.

Once when the television was on, Daddy wanted to see a program on another station. He very seriously asked, "Does anyone know how to change the station on this set?" Everyone laughed. We thought he was teasing, but he did not have a television in prison on which he could choose a program. My father-in-law changed the station, and Daddy seemed amazed that he was able to change the station on an unfamiliar set.

Daddy loves to cook. Once he began cooking a special concoction of eggs, sausage, potatoes and onions. He named it, along with everything else for which he couldn't think of a name, "Ho-Jo." Daddy began to get up everyday at dawn, much to Mother's dismay, and cook "Ho-Jo." My brother Billie, Jr., and Daddy loved to go into the kitchen and cook "Ho-Jo" for Billie's high school friends for breakfast. Daddy and Billie even began calling each other "Ho-Jo."

On Daddy's first birthday back at home I called from Houston to wish him a happy birthday, and my youngest sister Joy answered the phone. She said Mother and Daddy had gone out to eat Mexican food. I asked Joy how old Daddy was. She said Daddy said he was 40. I began adding my age of 24 to his age when I was born, and I knew he had to be at least 45. Then Joy explained Daddy's reasoning to me. Daddy said he was 40 (instead of the actual 47) because "somewhere along the line he had lost seven years."

The gift my brother gave Daddy was symbolic of the humor

which Daddy and my brother share. Billie gave Daddy a gold money clip engraved "The Ho-Jo King."

Since we hadn't been able to buy gifts for Daddy in so long, we had fun selecting presents for him. We bought him doubleknit slacks, tapered body shirts in psychedelic prints, wide ties and mod belts. Daddy's brother John, who had been like a father to us while Daddy was away, gave him an outdoor barbecue pit.

On Christmas Eve Daddy put on his Santa Claus suit, which had been in moth balls in Mother's famous banana boxes ("just the right size for storing Daddy's clothes," she says). He went with Mother to deliver gifts to two families. Mother bought a poodle puppy for one of her friends. We put the tiny puppy in a large box, put a ribbon on it and took it to her friend's home. We sang, "We wish you a merry Christmas," outside her door. When she opened her front door, we all trouped in and presented her with the puppy. She named the puppy "Estes," and Daddy said, "I don't know why you would want to do a thing like that to such an innocent little puppy. This name hasn't been very lucky for me." Two weeks later, she returned the puppy to Mother and Daddy and said it was just too much trouble to care for. Mother and Daddy kept the puppy and Daddy named him, naturally, "Ho-Jo." Mother said she already had enough "Ho-Jos" around the house. Finally, Daddy renamed it "Pepi."

We had Christmas Eve dinner with Uncle John L. and his family. We stood in a circle as Daddy led the prayer, and with tear-filled eyes thanked God for bringing us together again. There were many times during those years when we almost lost hope that we would be together at Christmas again.

After a Texas-style meal of chili and tamales, which is traditional on Christmas evening in our family, my sister Dawn's fiancee, now her husband, played his guitar and sang country-western music.

Daddy told stories as Danny played "Folsum Prison Blues," and "Green, Green Grass of Home" and "Blacktop County Chain."

The day after Christmas, we called Daddy's parole officer to get permission for him to go to Houston with us for a visit. Daddy received permission, but the further he got from Abilene and home, the more nervous he became. He said it was like a dream. He couldn't believe he was actually with us on a pleasure trip, not handcuffed in a federal car.

It was difficult for him to realize that the kids were adults, married and living in homes of their own.

Daddy began to relax as he watched the countryside from Abilene to Austin to Houston. When we passed the Astrodome in Houston, Daddy was fascinated by the development of an area which was just a pasture 10 years before. He quipped to Mother, "Pat, I told you I should have bought up that land back in 1960."

While Daddy was at our apartment, he went with my husband to walk our dog, Katy. They met the gardener for our apartment, and Walter introduced him to Daddy. By habit, Daddy extended his right hand to the man and said, "I'm Billie Sol Estes. How do you do?" The gardener's eyes lit up, and he said, "You ain't that big convict named Billie Sol Estes is you?" Daddy said, "That's right, they just turned me loose."

When Daddy meets a past acquaintance or friend, they very carefully avoid mentioning that he has been in prison until he puts them at ease by laughing and saying, "You know, it surely is great to be out of jail."

While Daddy was in Houston, we went to church and our preacher invited us to his house for coffee after the services. Daddy was on a tear that night. Our preacher was attending law school part-time, and Daddy started talking about dishonest lawyers. He quipped, "All lawyers are crooks, and it takes a crook to know one." I nearly died from embarrassment.

X CHAPTER

Wheeler-Dealers and Their Rolexes

One of the conditions of Daddy's parole was that he must take a job approved by his parole officer. The job he had at the time of his release was managing Uncle John L.'s pig farm. That, predictably, didn't last long. Daddy and Uncle John L. soon replaced the pigs with cows, left them to fend for themselves, and Daddy came into Abilene to work for Ray Horton.

Ray Horton was a Midland oil man who was something of a wheeler-dealer like Daddy. He had real estate interests all over the state and he flew around the country in his own plane. He and Daddy had known each other many years ago, before Daddy's troubles began. So, when he bought Permian Petroleum in Abilene, it was like a lightning rod to Daddy, and it now seemed pre-ordained that he would go to work for Ray.

The terms of Daddy's parole forbade him to work as a promoter, so he took a job with Permian Petroleum as dispatcher. It wasn't long until Daddy became Ray's right-hand man. There was not much question at that point that Daddy was engaged in promotion, but forbidding a promoter to promote is like forbidding a fish to swim.

The *Dallas Morning News* quoted an unnamed former employer of Daddy's who said, "It was always a laughing matter that he was a radio dispatcher and part-time janitor," he said, "I never saw him on the radio or pushing a broom. He had a pretty swanky office and was always hotshotting around."

After Daddy went to work for Ray, Ray began acquiring other assets. In Abilene, Horton bought an office building on the southside of town and then purchased a large apartment complex nearby. The office building was to be their Abilene base.

Ray then acquired the Vagabond Motel in Houston and a large track of land near Houston Intercontinental Airport as well as a tract near the Dallas/Ft. Worth Airport. Ray also acquired a large ranch in central Texas and a hospital near Lubbock. In fact, he was beginning to build a large empire. I think it's fair to attribute a good bit of that rapid growth to his association with Daddy.

Meanwhile, back in Abilene, Ray leased a restaurant called La Posada which my mother managed for him. We all worked there at one time or another. My sisters and I worked as waitresses and Mother worked as cashier. Mother did a daily report, sent the money to Ray, and Ray would then write checks to the suppliers. We had trouble making money there because whenever anybody would come in that Daddy knew, he would insist that they not be charged for their meal. We had two banquet—size tables that were for family and friends, so anyone who sat there didn't pay.

La Posada did a very good business because the food and service were so good and the atmosphere friendly; however, because Daddy was giving away so much food, it still wasn't making money. So one day Daddy ordered Mother to double all the prices on the menu. Suddenly, people who were accustomed to paying $2.50 for an order of enchiladas were confronted with a bill for $5.00. Business dropped off very rapidly.

Mother continued to struggle on with the restaurant. If the cook didn't show up, or a waitress or dishwasher was out, we would all pitch in and help no matter what needed to be done. This high pressure routine finally caused Mother to have a breakdown, and she had to go into the hospital. Then I took over management of the restaurant, and after about seven weeks I collapsed and had to go to the hospital as well. And so La Posada was closed.

My husband, Walter, went to work briefly for Ray Horton and Daddy at that time, but that didn't work out very well. I remember when Walter quit. Daddy had asked Walter to get on the WATS line and call every Cadillac dealer in the United States and get a quote on a new El Dorado. Walter worked three days making those calls and just as he was getting his last quote, Daddy walked in and announced that he had just bought an El Dorado from the dealer across the street, and that was the day Walter told them to shove it. A few weeks earlier, Daddy had asked him to trace all the piplines in the United States on a map, but, by the time he had finished, Daddy had forgotten that he wanted the information. That was what it was like working for Daddy. He might have you spend days doing all the legwork on a project, and, by the time you had finished, he was off in another direction.

Meanwhile, Ray Horton developed a drinking problem and was not taking care of business as well as he had in the past. He had been very good to us, giving Mother one of their older Oldsmobiles and buying a new Cadillac for Daddy as part of his salary, but, nevertheless, his checks to suppliers at the restaurant began bouncing, and we began to get the flack for it because everybody thought it really belonged to us.

Things then began to get very tense between Ray and Daddy. Daddy tried to encourage him to go to Alcoholics Anonymous and to work out his family problems, but things just got worse. So, Daddy asked his parole officer, Claude Roach, to let him switch jobs. He had had two or three good job offers, but the parole board turned him down. Daddy's parole supervision was a farce and gave him no help, direction, counseling or rehabilitation. The parole officer was just interested in filling out his report and not being bothered by any real concerns of the parolee.

The only help they gave was to look the other way when they knew he was promoting and dealing, a violation of his parole. However, that was no great service to him since, later, that was the basis for revoking his parole. If they had intervened early, the situation might not have developed into a serious problem requiring revocation of parole.

The family dogs had formed their own opinions of the parole officer. Whenever Mr. Roach would appear at the house unexpectedly to make a spot check, the German shepherd Puzon would bite him going in and the poodle "Pepi" would bite him going out. Daddy soon got an official letter ordering him to get rid of the dogs. I don't recall that those dogs ever bit anybody except Mr. Roach.

NOT LONG AFTER DADDY WENT TO WORK for Ray, a man named Glen Hutson and his wife Wanda arrived in Abilene and went straight to Daddy. Glen and Daddy had been in Leavenworth together. Glen had grown up in Abilene, been a football star at Hardin-Simmons University, and, he told Daddy, he and Wanda had returned to Abilene to start a program for ex-convicts and he wanted Daddy's help. They started a program called "Prisoners' Personal Aid" and that was the one time when Daddy was beaten at his own game—in fact, the whole family was taken.

I was hired as a part-time social worker along with one other woman. We rented an office and were going to start a halfway house. "Prisoners' Personal Aid" had had a very successful program in Houston which had been running for several years. We checked their reputation with the Federal Bureau of Prisons, and they recommended them highly. We called Austin and got a similar recommendation. Then we went to their annual fundraising dinner in Houston and were very impressed. The Wilburn Brothers from Nashville provided the entertainment.

We worked for six months and never got any funding or pay although they continued to assure us that everything was okay. In addition to myself and the other social worker, my husband, who had a masters degree in Human Relations, had been spending considerable amounts of time counseling ex-convicts.

Finally, we received paychecks. By that time they owed me about $10,000, and, as soon as I got my check, I deposited it and began writing checks to pay all my bills. The check very soon came bouncing back from the bank and I had to quickly borrow money from my father-in-law to keep my own checks from bouncing. The next thing that happened was that the Hutsons disappeared, and it was left to me to call all the office equipment rental places to come pick up typewriters and Xerox machines.

Unfortunately, Glen and Wanda Hutson were not atypical of the people who began calling on Daddy when he was released from prison. They were just part of a steady stream of people. It seemed that at least once a week a rented limousine would roll up to our door bearing people like Glen with plans and schemes. The limousine rentals were probably paid for with hot checks. Unfortunately, so many of these people were plausible, and at least some of them were potentially legitmate.

After the Glen and Wanda experience, Uncle John L. began to get very concerned that Daddy was eventually going to get hurt by one of these people. He also felt Daddy was "flying a little too high" as he put it, wearing Las Vegas type clothes bought for him by Ray Horton, the two of them running around the country, wearing matching mink hats.

I became concerned about Daddy a couple of years earlier when I was living in Houston and newly married. One time when Daddy and Ray came to Houston to visit Ray's motel, I went to meet them. They had a very pretty woman with them who they introduced as Ray's secretary. I was so naive at the time that I thought she really was a secretary, and since I was working as a semi-secretary myself, I tried to engage her in a little secretary talk only to find out that she didn't seem to be familiar with things secretarial or have any knowledge of Ray's business. I looked over at Daddy and suddenly became worried. I remembered numerous times before when they had traveled together with extra secretarial help. But Daddy and Ray were having such a good time that I was glad to be able to watch him be happy and enjoy himself.

THERE WERE MANY PEOPLE, ESPECIALLY ambitious young men, who thought Daddy could teach them how to get rich. There was a whole parade of these people who offered to work for nothing, or almost nothing to be around him and study his methods.

One of these young men was Don Wright. He had a beautiful young wife, Mickey, and had little money but lots of ambition. He became Daddy's and Ray Horton's pilot, and for a while Mickey was Daddy's secretary.

Don Wright later acquired some oil leases in a lottery, gathered together some more leases, struck oil and became one of the richest men in Abilene. I think the time he spent with Daddy paid off for him.

It was Don who introduced Daddy to Sue Goolsby. Sue had been unit manager for Hertz at the Abilene airport and had gotten to know Don. She would say to him whenever she would see him, "Don, when are you going to introduce me to some of these rich men you fly around all the time?"

Don asked, "Well, who do you want to meet?"

"Somebody famous and rich," Sue replied. And so Don said, "Well, how about Billie Sol?" and Sue then said, "Okay, I'll cook you a steak dinner if you'll introduce me to Billie Sol."

Sue Goolsby became Daddy's secretary and good friend. Sue remained loyal to Daddy even after she was indicted as part of the government's plot to blackmail Daddy into a plea bargain. Charges against her were dropped the day her trial was to begin.

As far back as I can remember, Daddy has always had a secretary. They all seemed to be very efficient and devoted. Daddy seems to have that effect on people. The secretary who was working for him at the time of his first arrest had a breakdown when his case broke. Another secretary, a glamorous blonde, gave me my first glimpse of marital infidelity when I was just a child. We had gone to see Daddy off at the Midland/Odessa airport and there was Daddy's secretary sitting in the restaurant with a strange man. I was puzzled because Daddy seemed to ignore them. I wanted to rush over to them and greet her, which seemed like the natural thing to do, but Daddy said, "No. Leave them alone and let them eat their breakfast." I was an adult before I figured out Daddy's strange behavior that day.

Daddy is the kind of person who has to have a detail person on hand every minute of the day. I was that person until I moved to Houston. When Sue Goolsby went to work for him, she filled that role. Sue was in complete charge of the details of his life as well as her other duties. She performed these tasks so well that she soon became indispensable.

When Daddy and Sue became constant companions out in the community and at dinner as well as lunch, I began to get concerned about how it would affect Mother. It was during this period that Mother had a complete physical and nervous breakdown from overwork at La Posada. I suspect that Daddy's relationship with Sue was at least partially responsible, but to this day, Mother and I have not discussed it. Nor have Daddy and I talked about it.

It was shortly after Daddy and Sue began being seen together that one of the Abilene congregations of the Church of Christ called together its elders and summoned Uncle John L. to discuss Daddy's disfellowship, which is the Church of Christ word for excommunication. When they confronted Daddy with their decision, he simply told them that he wasn't a member of that particular congregation so their edict was meaningless. A man at church had a hopeless crush on my mother and sent her flowers and candy constantly. Mother was oblivious to his attentions and may even have been unaware that they were more than just friendly gestures. After all, if you're married to Billie Sol Estes, you don't have time for any more problems.

SUE WORKED FOR RAY AND DADDY MORE than five years and her most important contribution to our well-being was to fend off the crazier of the crazies who had begun to invade our lives the minute Daddy got out of prison. When I first became aware of Daddy's and Sue's affair I had very mixed feelings. I was glad to see Daddy happy, but I had very old fashioned ideas about the marriage vow and I was worried about how it would affect my Mother. For an old fashioned woman like Mother, divorce is not in the vocabulary, so she looked the other way.

Nevertheless, Daddy's relationship with Sue was important to him. I'm sure it was important for Sue as well. Both Daddy and Sue are very reticent about talking about their time together—as might be expected. However, Sue has shared some lighthearted moments with me that she recalls from those years.

She particularly remembers one special trip. It was close to Christmas and Ray and his girlfriend, Daddy and Sue took off for Las Vegas. Daddy had to get permission from his parole officer to leave Abilene. He was going to Las Vegas to help Ray Horton close a big deal with Phillips Petroleum. Since the holiday was so near, when they checked into Caesar's Palace, Ray bought his girlfriend a leather coat and bought some gold charms for his daughters.

Daddy had no interest in gambling and seemed puzzled by what was going on in the casinos. Ray, however, took to the casino like a baby to a bottle and even won some money playing baccarat.

In the evening they went to the casino show, which Daddy slept through. Phyllis Diller was the star. Daddy, truly puzzled, asked Sue just before he dropped off to sleep in his seat, "Is she supposed to be pretty?"

Later, they got into a hotel elevator with Telly Savalas. He turned to Daddy and said, "Hi, I'm Telly Savalas of *Kojak.*" Daddy stuck out his hand and replied, "How do you do. I'm Billie Sol Estes of Texas." Everyone in the elevator laughed.

Sue remembers that before they had been at the hotel half a day, Daddy was paged on the hotel's public address system. When word got out that Billie Sol was in Vegas, he was paged every few minutes by people he knew from everywhere. Ray seemed a little put out.

After their visit to the casino, Daddy seemed to be carefully observing all the people around him. He turned to Sue, and without any trace or irony, said, "There sure seems to be a lot of men here with their daughters."

NOT LONG AGO, SUE AND I HAD A GOOD laugh about the time her cat, Mafia, died. She was very upset, she remembered. It had been a faithful companion for many years, so she cried about it a lot. Then she called Daddy and he came over to comfort her. "I know what that cat has meant to you, Sue," Daddy said. "So I'm going to see that it gets a decent dignified burial." He wrapped it in a towel and put it into a laundry basket. "Don't you worry about a thing. I'm going to take it out to the lake behind the house and bury it."

This is the kind of chore that Daddy normally would have had Fred Michaelis, his chauffeur do, but since it was Sue's cat, he did it himself. He found a shovel and dug a deep hole in a shady spot near the lake and buried the cat just as he had promised. Daddy recalls, "The next day, there were a half dozen Feds out there in the back with shovels. They had dug up that old cat and half the back yard."

MOTHER'S AND DADDY'S PHONES HAD BEEN bugged for some time, as were the phones of many people they knew. Daddy and his friends had a running telephone joke for the benefit of eavesdroppers. "I'm about out of money," Sue would tell Daddy over the phone, "You better go out and dig some up."

Toward the end, just before Daddy was entrapped by the Feds, Sue gave up and returned to live with her mother in Lubbock. She told me recently, "I was tired and emotionally drained. I couldn't stand what was happening to Billie."

When the Feds came to Lubbock to try to recruit her as a witness against Daddy, they came, they thought, with strong inducements. If she wouldn't testify, they would charge her with conspiracy to conceal assets, right along with Daddy. Whenever they would come to see her, they would repeatedly tell her that she was going to jail. "I had been working 90 hours a week, my mother was sick, my son had just gone to jail, and my house had burned down; and they kept saying to me, '30 years, 30 years for conspiracy.' I damned near said to them, 'I'll take it. I hear those ladies' prisons have tennis courts, swimming pools and free medical care.' If they thought they were scaring me by offering to take me away from my troubles for 30 years, they were using the wrong strategy."

Sue continued to refuse to testify. "There wasn't anything to testify about," she said. "You know how boys are. When it comes time to have serious talks about business, they send the girls to make coffee. Well, I just didn't have any evidence to give." The day Sue's trial was to begin in Federal court in Dallas, the charges were dropped. The reason they were dropped was because Daddy hired James Linn's law firm in Oklahoma City to represent Sue. Until that point, the prosecutors had planned to run her through a trial, get a quick and easy conviction and send her to jail. When James Linn began subpoenaing witnesses and filing discovery motions, the prosecutions reluctantly admitted that they didn't have a case and dropped the charges.

Walter and I moved back to Abilene from Houston in 1973.

Shortly before that, Walter's dad had walked into our townhouse fresh from a trip to Germany and informed Walter that he had sold his inheritance, the Foster Cathead Company. Walter was immediately fired, so Ray Horton offered him a job working with Daddy. Daddy was the typical father-in-law who is inclined to be hard on his daughter's husbands. He would never praise Walter for anything, no matter how deserving, and Walter was deserving many times. It was Walter who was always available to drive Daddy to Dallas to hearings or wherever else he needed to go, and it was Walter who often picked up the check when the whole family went out to dinner. Daddy's one compliment to Walter was during one of our many trips to Dallas during the plea-bargain negotiations after Daddy had been threatened with new indictments. Walter was driving our Mercedes, as he always did, and I could tell that Daddy wanted to say something complimentary to Walter, because despite his reluctance to praise him, I knew Daddy loved him very much.

Finally, after being silent for a long time Daddy said, "You know Walt, you would have made a good race car driver."

BILLY PYRON WAS ONE OF THE ENDLESS stream of promoters seeking out Daddy who passed Sue's inspection and got into see him. That first meeting resulted in Billy's buying a chain of CB-radio stores in Abilene, named Frenchman's Creek. Billy was a sharp promoter himself, who had married a rich Tyler heiress, and at that time was on a roll in Abilene. It was soon after that when he gave Sue Goolsby his power of attorney so she could sign for him at real estate closings and save him from having to come to Abilene every time he closed a deal. He was later to deny on the witness stand having signed the letter giving her that authority. Fortunately for Sue, she had saved the original letter, and hand writing experts confirmed

Billy's signature.

THEN DON TRULL APPEARED ON THE SCENE. When I say appeared, I mean just that. None of the endless stream of wheeler-dealers wrote ahead or called to see if they might be welcomed or needed. They just showed up one after another. Anyway, that's how Don Trull came into our lives. He was simply there one day sitting in Daddy's office. I don't remember where he said he came from or how he knew Daddy, or even if he did know Daddy. He claimed to have known Daddy from years back. Daddy didn't seem to remember him, yet I don't see how anyone would ever forget knowing Don Trull or want to repeat the experience.

At that time I was running a plant store and antique shop and selling real estate in one of the stores in Ray's building. We had been having some trouble with a leaking roof, and Don climbed right up on the roof to look it over. The first thing he did was to take a broom and sweep off all the puddles of water standing on the roof. Then he got some hot tar and patched the leaks. We were very impressed. He was off to a good start. When Daddy found out he didn't have any place to stay or any money, he hired him to do maintenance and told him he could stay in one of the empty offices in the building. He moved in immediately with his two sons, one age 11 and one age 14. He said his wife would come out later.

Don Trull takes up a lot of space in this story, not because any of us were fond of him, but because he caused such a lot of trouble and was largely responsible for Daddy's return to jail. The best insight into the character of the man who was to cause so much havoc in our lives is from a story told by Steve, the former owner of the Airport Lounge at the Abilene airport. Steve says, "Don Trull first came in my restaurant for coffee in January, 1977. He seemed like a nice guy.

He came in several times and sat for hours. He asked me, 'How come you don't have a lounge?' I said, 'I don't have the money, but plan to open one later.' "

"Don said he would finance it if I made him a 50 percent partner. He asked for copies of my lease and my resume of past work, and he took them and photostated them and then returned them to me.

"He then began getting estimates on putting in a lounge. He called a carpet store for carpet. (I cancelled this when I realized he was not going to pay for it. It was too late to cancel some of the other stuff.) He called a glass company and told them he owned the Airport Lounge and ordered glass doors and mirrors. Then the glass company called and said they had a bill for $2,400, and they could not put in the rest of the mirrors without some payment. (I think they had read about Don Trull in the newspaper.) Also, a bar was built by some carpenters, and I don't know who they were, and I have not been contacted yet for the money, but I expect to probably hear from them.

"Mr. Trull told me he was rich. He said he owned many corporations and showed me many papers. He said he could get financing for me and asked me if he could sign his tickets. From January to March he charged $1,500 worth of food for himself and his friends. He signed tickets like a big shot. One time he had a suitcase with a lot of cash in it.

"He said he owned steam cleaners and he was going to sell them in Iran, and I overheard him trying to get people to invest in his steam machines. He told me he owned Frenchman's Creek Electronics. He said he just bought it."

It was very much in character for Don Trull to claim ownership of any enterprise where he worked. There's no telling where he got a suitcase full of money, but that is completely in character for him.

He would very soon begin claiming that Daddy and Billy Pyron owed him $1.5 million.

Frenchman's Creek CB store was located next door to my plant store. The CB business had been booming, and this was just before the CB bust—that point where everybody who was going to get a CB radio had already gotten one.

Mother and Daddy had met in Sunday School a man named Jap Burkett. Jap had listed his ranch for sale with Solex, our real estate office. His wife, Barbara, and my mother became close friends. In fact, they went on a tour together to the Holy Lands. Jap Burkett was looking for an investment in an Abilene business, so Daddy introduced him to Billy Pyron who was looking for someone to invest in his CB business. Burkett invested a total of $50,000 into the business, and Pyron hired Don Trull to run it.

It was soon after Jap Burkett made his investment and Don Trull became manager that the store failed and had to be closed. Don Trull then moved to Tyler to continue working for Billy Pyron.

Jap Burkett began yelling for Daddy to make his loss good. If he had gone after Billy Pyron, who owned the business, he might have had some chance of recovering his money, but instead, because it was Daddy, Burkett's Abilene attorney started yelling fraud and tried to recover from Daddy. He later recanted and admitted that Daddy hadn't defrauded him, but not before causing a great deal of grief.

At the same time, Don Trull was desperate for money. Someone broke into Daddy's office, gathered up all of the papers they could steal and made copies of them. Then Trull started trying to blackmail us. He had copies of all of Daddy's deals that had never worked out but that the parole board wouldn't be able to ignore if they were to see them.

My husband was teaching school when Don Trull turned up at his classroom and called him out and tried to extort money from him. When that didn't work, he called me and said, "I know which kindergarten your little girl goes to. If you don't get me some money she's gonna' get a ride home with someone you don't want her to ride with."

We didn't submit to his threats, so he kept his word and mailed all Daddy's papers to the FBI, the IRS, the parole board and everybody else he thought could damage Daddy.

Ray Horton's businesses continued to decline, so Daddy got Dr. Lindley from Pecos, an old friend, to buy the Horton building. In the meantime, my husband and I found a building on the North side of town and opened another real estate office.

Exit Don Trull to Tyler. When he got to Tyler he very quickly got up to his old tricks and began trying to get money out of Billy Pyron much as he had tried with us. This time he went a little further. He went to Pyron's penthouse office and poured gasoline over all the furniture and then held Pyron's assistant, Billy May, at gunpoint. He demanded $10,000 and a red Cadillac in exchange for not shooting May and not setting fire to the building. Billy Pyron was no more susceptible to extortion than we were, so Don Trull ended up in jail on a charge of kidnapping and attempted murder. (This story shouldn't have anything to do with the Estes family, but ironically it led us to someone who was later to be very important to us—Jerry Irwin).

The only smart thing Don Trull did during the time we knew him was to hire Jerry Irwin as his defense attorney. The first thing Jerry did for his new client was to subpoena everybody who had ever heard of Don Trull to testify at his trial. This sowed confusion to such an extent that the jury did not convict him. About 50 people were subpoenaed. They even subpoenaed an elderly real estate salesman who had worked for me and had no connection with the case whatever. He hadn't had a new suit in years, so he went out and bought one for the circus in Tyler. I think it was the most exciting thing that had ever happened to him.

XI CHAPTER

The Little Peacock

This was to be our second circus in Tyler. Irwin's defense very soon became clear. Since Don Trull had once been associated with the notorious Billie Sol Estes, he would subpoena Daddy, all his family and associates and create such confusion that the jury would very soon forget who was on trial or for what.

The Dallas Morning News on April 2, 1978 described it as follows. "The courtroom appearance of paroled swindler Billie Sol Estes as a witness in a kidnapping trial here almost snatched newspaper headlines from the defendent, Estes' former business partner, Don Trull. But that may have been just what defense attorney G. Brockett Irwin of Longview had in mind when he subpoenaed Estes and almost 55 other witnesses, most with Estes connections and many of whom never took the stand."

The article went on to report that IRS agents who were

investigating Daddy came to court and sat quietly in the back of the room, perhaps hoping that Daddy would come clean on the stand and reveal where all that hidden money has been buried in the last 20 years.

At the trial, Trull claimed that Daddy and Billy Pyron cheated him out of $1.5 million. And remember, this is supposed to be a trial about Don Trull kidnapping a man and threatening to kill him. Of course, the prosecutor objected a lot, and the judge upheld the objections a lot, but neither was quite up to Jerry Irwin. He claimed he was trying to prove that Don Trull was just trying to collect a lawful debt.

The astonishing thing to me about the trial was that Don Trull was acquitted. Even though I was convinced from the evidence that Trull had kidnapped the man and threatened to kill him, Irwin managed to implant a sufficient amount of doubt into the minds of the jurors that they didn't take long to find him innocent.

The trial was very frustrating for us because Don Trull had already caused us lots of trouble, and his charade of a trial was too much for me to bear. Once during the trial I muttered that Trull was a son-of-a-bitch. I must have muttered louder than I thought because before I knew it, Irwin was demanding that I be jailed for contempt.

The judge reprimanded me with a smile. I had a feeling that he agreed with me about Trull. He said, "Did you call Mr. Trull an S.O.B.?" I said, "I didn't just call him one, he is one." We returned home that night, and the next morning I had several calls from people who had heard on the radio that I had almost been put in jail. I was then surprised to hear that they had mentioned it on "Good Morning America" and the "Today" show.

When we returned to Tyler for the resumption of the trial, we ran into Don Trull at the Sheraton, where we were all staying. He had lost a lot of weight, had his hair dyed dark brown and up in a pancake and was wearing a respectable looking business suit. I think Irwin did a good job changing his image. He was even lacking his big cigar and cowboy hat.

Later on, Irwin recalls meeting Daddy at that trial. "He was nothing like I expected. I expected a very smooth con artist but instead saw an unpretentious businessman. He looked like an unmade bed, anything but smooth. You have to get to know him well to detect his genius. After you get to know him, it is laughable that he is a con artist."

I was still very angry at Jerry Irwin. We had been subpoenaed as witnesses for someone who had done us irreparable harm at great expense to us. However, Jack Bryant, our attorney, reminded me, "It is the right of the defendant to have his defense," whether we were willing to come or not."

There were 32 people questioned the first day of jury selection, and they were all disqualified for one reason or another. Then in a surprise move, Irwin decided to take the next 12—no matter who they were or how they answered the questioning. I didn't understand why he was doing that unless he was trying to get some kind of grounds for a mistrial later. When the witnesses were called, the "circus-like" atmosphere began.

The jury never knew what was going on during that trial. They were out of the courtroom more than they were in, because of Bills of Exception, which allows testimony to be presented to the judge without the jury's presence.

Sue Goolsby was one of the star witnesses at that trial. She was one of the many people Trull had tried to blackmail. Also, he had called her mother, Mrs. McClendon, in Lamesa, Texas, and told her that her daughter was "going to jail." He was referring to Pyron's claim that Sue had forged Pyron's name on a loan document and didn't have his power of attorney. The power of attorney letter became one of the hottest pieces of evidence at the trial even though it was totally irrelevant.

Sue was also questioned about her relationship with Daddy. She said, "It is very close. I've never known anyone like him before. He has been good to me, good to my mother, and was good to my father." Sue broke into tears at this point. Her father had been ill, and she had also put off having a cancer biopsy so she could be at the Tyler trial.

Our attorney was there both as a witness and as Daddy's legal representative. Jack kept counseling me to "be a lady" and not show my hostility to Trull. After having been threatened by him with kidnapping our daughters and having him try to extort money from everyone we know, it was going to be a hard job not to be openly hostile to him.

Billy May, the man who claimed to have been held at gunpoint and threatened with burning by Trull, should have been the star witness. But he was completely overshadowed by the defense witnesses. Billy wore the same green suit each day and had a rather sallow complexion.

Trull claimed that May was not really harmed and that he had even given him the opportunity to go down the hall to a restroom, but May testified that when he needed to use the restroom three times, Trull made him use a coffee urn. Trull repeatedly said, in a tape played by the prosecution, that he just "wanted his money." If Trull ever had any money he sure managed to keep it hidden while he was in Abilene. After he moved out of Ray Horton's office building, he stayed in two Abilene motels and couldn't pay his bill and was charged with theft of services. He then moved into a house in Clyde, never madc a payment, and we had to evict him. That was the time he began threatening us.

Wray Cure was perhaps the most colorful of the witnesses. While we were waiting for our turn to go on, Wray passed his time writing a philosophical thesis in a very artistic handwriting. He had been shot two years before, he says by the Mafia, and his Windmill Properties empire collapsed when he was given some phony bearer bonds on a multi-million dollar transaction in Houston. His mother was mysteriously shot in bed in Abilene, and his father served time in Huntsville for the crime, which many people believe he didn't commit. Wray repeatedly said he didn't know why he had been subpoenaed, but the defense had a surprise for him; they asked him if it was true that he had offered a man named Frank Head $500 to kill Don Trull. Cure denied it and Irwin threatened to charge him with perjury and conspiracy to commit murder. As word of his testimony got around the witness room, several of us jokingly considered offering to chip in to help Cure defray the expense of getting rid of Trull. Irwin never followed through with his threat, and Cure left for Houston to close a big apartment deal.

After a colorful summation by Jerry Irwin, the jury retired and found Don Trull not guilty. We were all shocked at the verdict, but Daddy said, "Jerry Irwin is the kind of lawyer I have always needed."

XII CHAPTER

Blackmail and Conspiracy

In the parade of people who trooped in to see Daddy while he was at Permian Petroleum, not all were con artists and wheeler-dealers. Some of them were undercover agents for the FBI or for the IRS. In the summer of 1977, after Sue had returned to Lubbock and there was nobody to screen visitors, Daddy received a contingent of about seven people. Sue would have spotted them immediately. I felt there was something wrong with them, but Daddy didn't trust my judgment. The head of this team introduced himself as Walter Placko and said he was looking for investments. His real name was Walter Perry and he was an IRS investigator.

One evening I went with Mother and Daddy out to dinner with Walter Placko. He had an unattractive woman with him who posed as his mistress but who really was an IRS agent. I was suspicious because their relationship did not appear to be that of lovers. Placko pretended to be wealthy, but didn't even know how or what to order in a good restaurant. He didn't seem to know what wine went with the blue plate special. Also, his mistress didn't seem to know about hairdressers and manicurists, not to mention dressmakers or jewelers. I remember telling Daddy I didn't care for the people, and that they obviously weren't wealthy. But, at that time, I supposed he was just one of that army of would-be wheeler-dealers who had been showing up in rented limousines since Daddy got out of jail. We had gotten so used to that that we didn't take them very seriously.

However, these two were wired for sound and with their body mikes and telephone taps and other bugs made 30 hours of tapes of Daddy's personal and intimate conversations.

Later, they took Daddy to a business meeting at a motel and gave him something to drink, and considering the bold way he talked on the tapes, they must have given him drugs as well. They made Daddy a phony proposition for a business deal. Since Daddy fell for it, even though it was never consumated, they claimed later at the trial that it proved that he was making big business deals and hiding the money. The tapes the jury found incriminating were made at that session.

In a recording dated July 20, 1977, and played for the jury, Daddy said, "After all the trouble that I've ever been in, my credibility is good as hell. I am going to make something of the profit. And I am going to run, and I'm not in a position that we can be sued or in a lawsuit for not fulfilling our obligations. 'Cause I'll be on my way back to jail, and I cannot have any trouble, you understand."

Daddy's voice was slurred on the recording. At one point he is heard to say, "He will goddamn sure sign the contract or I'll kill the son-of-a-bitch on the spot." Then some time later he said, "Don't ever fuck with my goddamn money." I am convinced that Daddy was drugged when that tape was made. The language he uses is very uncharacteristic of him. It makes him seem almost a Jeckle and Hyde character.

A few days after the agents made their tapes, Daddy called a number he had been given by Placko. The person answering the phone obviously was unaware of the undercover operation. He answered, "Internal Revenue Service." Daddy said, "Oh, shit," and hung up.

Once we became aware that federal investigators were after Daddy again, we began to try to plan intelligently how we could counter them, how we could prepare a defense, given the fact that we had very little money to work with. One of the wiser precautions Daddy took was to get Fred Michaelis to help him set up recording equipment on the phones. That way, potential prosecution witnesses could be called on the phone, engaged in a conversation in which they talked about the case. Later, they could be confronted with tapes of the conversations to make sure that they told the truth on the stand. It also helped in cross-examination.

We were aware at this point that all our phone conversations, as well as private meetings, had been recorded by the feds, so we wanted to have recordings of our own. That's why we were fortunate enough to have a transcript of the prosecutors conversation between Jim Rolfe and Jack Bryant that Daddy insists is blackmail. Normally a plea bargain is a guilty plea in exchange for a light sentence or a plea to a lesser charge. In this case the government's offer was neither of these but a threat to indict Daddy's whole family unless he pleaded guilty. He was furious.

They also threatened to indict Daddy's lawyer, Jack Bryant. Bryant was scared almost out of his skin. He had been a close family friend, a classmate of Uncle John L., and a long-time neighbor, and he had handled the family's legal work for years.

Bryant's indictable offense, according to the government, was that he helped set up a trust fund for us kids. It was the government's contention that that was a plot to conceal Daddy's assets to avoid tax liens.

And so, to add to all our other troubles, we were without a lawyer. This might be a minor problem to the ordinary person but it was almost impossible to find a lawyer who would represent Billie Sol Estes. In the first place, Daddy's lawyers must be totally without political ambitions. The path to high political office in Texas lies in prosecuting Billie Sol Estes, not in defending him.

Secondly, they must be truly fearless. What had happened to Jack Bryant would not be totally lost on any law firm considering representing Daddy. Federal prosecutors have leverage to use against defense representatives, the Jack Bryant indictment threat being just one example.

Thirdly, they need to be masochists. Defending Daddy is not always a popular sport. By the time Daddy's trial came around, about 95 percent of the general public believed that he was guilty because he had been convicted 15 years previously, and his name was a household word, meaning swindle. Therefore, the only reason any lawyer would represent him would be because he was money-hungry.

Which brings us to fourthly. The lawyers couldn't count on enriching themselves representing Daddy. While we all scraped the bottom of our purses to come up with money for a defense, it would never be enough to counter the million dollars being spent by the prosecution.

Clearly then, the defense representative must be someone who is brash and reckless, without too much to lose; insensitive to public opinion, with a spotless background that can stand the closest scrutiny by all kinds of federal agencies such as the FBI and IRS; a fighting tenacity; and at least the possibility of developing some sympathy for Daddy's situation.

My former brother-in-law thought Daddy should have Richard "Racehorse" Haynes as his legal representative. He felt more than a little responsible for part of Daddy's dilemma because it was he who got Daddy involved in the Frenchman's Creek CB business. Daddy, to save his son-in-law's job, got Billy Pyron to purchase the company, and that led to the Jap Burkett loan, the Sue Goolsby indictment, and much of the other grief and aggravation.

So, with some difficulty, a meeting was arranged with "Racehorse". The only time he could see Daddy was between flights at the Dallas/Fort Worth Airport. Daddy decided at the last moment to go to the meeting and so he had only about two hours to get from Abilene to the airport, a distance of about 150 miles. We jumped into the car, with myself at the wheel, and broke some speed laws. We got there just as Racehorse's plane pulled up to the gate. Haynes was a very attractive man, and it was easy to see why he always tried to get as many women as possible on his juries. When I told him I had been threatened with indictment, he put his hand on my arm and said, "Darling, they're never going to indict you. I know you never committed any crime." I felt his charm instantly.

We were very impressed with Haynes, but his fee would have been $50,000 plus considerable expenses. Daddy and I returned home and had another family meeting. To have met the costs of that kind of defense would have meant a second mortgage on everything every one of us owned plus considerable additional help from Uncle John L. Daddy decided that he just couldn't put his family through that kind of hardship in addition to everything else. We began to cast about for an alternative.

Daddy immediately thought of "the Little Peacock," Jerry Irwin. He reasoned that if Jerry could get Don Trull off on a charge he was so obviously guilty of, surely he could get Daddy off on a charge he was innocent of.

And so Daddy contacted Jerry. We had a big conference and all five kids chipped in $100 each, which was all the money we could come up with at that time. Uncle John L. managed to raise some more money later.

Irwin agreed to take the case. He was about five feet tall and not afraid of the devil himself. The first thing he did was to try to get the charges dropped on the grounds the government plea bargain was illegal.

Irwin contended in a brief submitted to U.S. Attorney General Griffin Bell that the plea bargain negotiations had been blackmail and that Jack Bryant as well as Jim Rolfe, had acted illegally.

The telephone transcript of the plea-bargain negotiations between Jack Bryant and Jim Rolfe, the prosecutor, tells the story.

Bryant: *As I told you the other day when we talked, I have recommended to Estes that since I am getting pretty close to this thing, personally, that probably he ought to have another lawyer look at it for him. He has done some looking like that. I am going to be in a position probably this afternoon that I have got to lay out a potential lawyer for him, and where we stand on the potential plea bargain that you and I talked about. Now, I have made myself a list of notes here that I am going to talk about. I'm going to tell him what is my understanding of it and to be sure that we are on firm ground, I want to run over it with you if you don't mind.*

Rolfe: *It suits me.*

B: *All right, I've got a page of notes just to be run down. Number one, we are looking at a potential of two separate indictments. The first one is basically a fraud indictment, involving mail fraud type things. This involves Mr. Horton, Mr. Estes, Ms. Goolsby, Mr. Copenhaver, Mr. Patterson, and Mr. Fuell. Mr. Fuell has pleaded guilty. I don't know what he pled guilty to.*

R: *He pled guilty to one count of Title 18 Section 13 Mail Fraud involving the steam cleaners to the three leasing companies.*

B: *O.K., well I didn't know that. As I understand, it involved Horton's steam cleaners . . .that was 1974. The first transaction involving Mr. Estes and Ms. Goolsby. . . forgeries within the Pyron Companies and something on the Concho Trade Schools. I don't know the details on that, but I assume it's of Peck Welders. And then the 2nd indictment is basically the Internal Revenue's indictment involving two basic types of allegations. One being conspiracy to conceal assets and the other being unreported income.*

R: *Right.*

B: *Initially the counts on the conspiracy to conceal assets involves Pam, John L., Jr., myself and Mr. Horton as well as Mr. Estes.*

R: *Right.*

B: *All right, the things that are involved in that are as far as general arrangement between Horton and Estes.*

R: *Right.*

B: *And that's basically what you're prepared to present to the Grand Jury.*

R: *Right.*

B: *And that our discussion was that #1 on the plea of guilty on one count of avoidance or concealment.*

R: *Which would be conspiracy.*

B: *Conspiracy. Conspiracy, generally involving Estes and Horton.*

R: *Right.*

B: *Right, in so far as with a plea of guilty on this by Estes, there would be no indictment of Pam, of John L., Jr., of me, or of Sue.*

R: *That would be my recommendation, that would be my recommendation based on a, you know, a, core, so to speak, of that conspiracy comprised of Mr. Horton and Mr. Estes and others mentioned to you being totally involved.*

B: *And then of course we would, as you and I discussed, make an offer of compromise to the government of doing something. . . basically trying to get $1 million toward the government, and I realize this is not your territory, but this is something we would like to do, to go ahead and get the civil liability (to satisfy the tax suit).*

R: *Well, I think it would be of benefit. . .*

B: *Alright, now then, on the one place that I am still a little bit in limbo on, is that, and. . ah. . I visited with Connard Florence a while this morning, a good while, just asking him what the ground rules really were, and I hadn't had time to talk to you about it. Within the Northern District I understand that you as attorneys don't make recommendations.*

R: That is true, they're never requested, and in fact. . . we. . ah. . we would. . you know. . be involved in difficulty. . . I believe Connard's words were roundly criticized.

B: Right. So basically all you can do is really control the number of counts that we're getting ready to go to trial on.

R: Control of exposure. That's true. That's what it is and. . . that is sometimes criticized.

B: I understand, that if we go on this, we still would have the liberty to offer to the court anything we wanted to in litigation or in question to sentencing.

B: Right. O.K.

R: We're out of the picture.

B: Right, once the plea is entered, why then its between us and the Judge.

R: Right.

B: AlL right, then the one place I'm in limbo on, Jim, is on the question of dealing with the Parole Commission. Now Sol is looking at, right now, if he were revoked, at oh, about 23 months still running on his parole.

R: Right.

B: Now, I don't frankly know what the law is if they revoked him. Whether he would have 23 months to do or whether he'd have 8 years to do.

R: Well, my understanding is that. . . .

B: I know what control you. . . .

R: Well, my understanding is that if he is revoked under certain conditions he would do the. . . he would go back to the day he got out.

B: Which would be the eight.

R: *Right, and under another set of circumstances he would do time now till the expiration.*

B: *All right, where do we go and who do I need to talk to to find out that set of circumstances and what the Parole Commission's reaction would be?*

R: *Well, now my understanding would be that. . . ah. . . you know, as we talked about it, I believe it was Sunday afternoon, the. . ah. . if it were agreed upon, I think it would be revoked one way or the other, so I think with everybody being fair and above board we're looking at a maximum exposure of 5 plus the. . .*

B: *Right.*

R: *I think we could. . . ah. . . I would agree that I would talk to the Parole Commission about minimizing the exposure to the extent that if there was revocation that it would be under conditions it would be now until the termination. . . which would mean that you would still have a shot at the trial committee. . . District Judge. . . which would run concurrently, but it may or may not.*

B: *I see.*

R: *So, I think you would be, you know, I mean my recommendation would be that it would be revoked, but you might as well roll the dice on it, but I think we could scale that down.*

B: *All right. I have not yet talked to Claude Roach. I wanted to get a little further along in this and. . . ah. . .*

R: *I'll talk to him. I'll give Dr. Amos a call in a few minutes. . . Obviously he has a little more authority.*

B: *Jim, would you do that, and find out because I think right now the place we're hanging, and of course there is going to be another lawyer representing Estes, which I think there should be.*

R: *Who is that going to be?*

B: *Well, I don't know; I would guess right now that it would be Dick Haynes. I talked to Estes this morning and he has not yet made a deal with anybody. He has talked to Dick Haynes, and it would be beautiful if you could get some idea, because I think this will be a controlling thing as to whether or not we're looking at. . . let's talk about outside exposure. Now, you've got age plus 5. There's a top end of 13, on the other hand, you're looking at the Parole Commission taking another position. We're looking at a 5 plus 2 or taking a 3rd position, we're looking at a maximum of a 5.*

R: *Right.*

B: *And, I think that if I were continuing to represent him, I would want to know that, and I feel sure that his lawyer that represents him would want to know which of those and if you've got a. . . stroke, I guess that would be the word, to be able to get some indication from Dr. Amos, it would sure help.*

R: *O.K. Well, I will, you know, call him and ask him what the alternatives are.*

B: *If you would, would you do that and call me back?*

R: *Jack are you going to be there a while?*

B: *I'll be in the office all afternoon.*

R: *O.K. I'll call you in a few minutes.*

B: *All right, that'll be fine. Thank you very much.*

R: *O.K. Bye.*

A few minutes later...

R: *Jack, listen I talked to Dr. Amos and. . . ah. . . he said that. . . ah. . . there would be a possiblity of a. . . ah. . . not the complete revocation that. . . ah. . . he would, you know, go along with. . . ah. . . the two. . . you know, just. . . ah. . . possibility of revoking probation. I mean the parole of two now to the time of the plea to the time of the expiration. . . that's the information.*

B: *O.K.*

R: *. . . which would minimize the hell out of it. All right, as far as that goes. . . now he recommends that he is one of eight commissioners, the way that would work, he has to get, you know, they're fairly autonomous, but he would. . . ah. . . have to get two commissioners to. . . ah. . . go along with that, and I don't see any problem with that because they. . . ah. . .*

B: *One more question, then, would be, assuming Dr. Amos could get it to work like he wants to, whether the judge would allow the sentence to begin now or whether he would box-car it and tie it with the existing sentence.*

R: *Well, that's what we have no idea of. The judge wouldn't tell us that.*

B: *That's where we are so, really we're looking at the possibility, outside possibility, of 7 down to whatever the judge wants to give out.*

R: *Yes.*

B: *That's where we are.*

R: *And, I'll tell you what I would, you know, what I would, you know, if we could get this thing wound up, which I'm obviously anxious to do, as well as everybody else. . .*

cause we're spending hundreds of dollars a day.

B: *Well, needless to say, I'm interested in getting it wound up, too. This is interfering in my law practice.*

R: *I can imagine everybody is. I would. . . ah. . . I would recommend. . . ah you know, to the Parole Board that they. . . ah. . . revoke his parole. . . ah. . . say for a year and scale that down to six, now that would be my recommendation. I think it would be. . . I think Dr. Amos would go along with that because he is tired of, you know, everything that's connected to this case too.*

B: *Now, Jim, let's talk about judges a moment.*

R: *Well, I'll tell you the. . . ah. . . you know, as I said the other day, the . . . ah. . . my personal feeling is if the venue was lying anywhere in the Northern District of Texas. . .*

B: *Of course, I don't even know all the judges in the division. I think basically Eldon Mahon is the favorite judge, and although I'm very fond of Leo Brewster, in the Estes case, I don't think he would be the proper judge, because. . .*

R: *Well, that's ah. . . you know. . . I really don't know, I wasn't around when all of that occurred, and all I do is. . . ah. . . you know to be fair about it, is to, like I say, ... and I'll tell you what though. . . I know y'all are conscientiously trying to reach a decision, but ah. . in us going back and forth, it has a. . . as you said, you have a law practice. I have too. I'm going to have to canvas. . . a really concentrated operation. . . what I would like to do is, now that the cards are pretty well on the table, is to. . . ah. . . I don't see anything else to influence your decision making process. . . now this will be separate and apart from the civil—that should wind everything up. . . you . . you can fight that battle. . . Now try not to make this contingent on any money. . .*

B: *That gives us a lot more leaveway because our trying to raise a million dollars is. . . even to super stroke folks. . . it takes time.*

R: *Sure it does. But it would be to his benefit if he ever wants to have. . . reach a status of a clean slate to work on that.*

B: *All right. What I'm going to do. . .*

R: *So excuse me, in the interest of that, you know, I've got other things to do this weekend, I've got other cases to work on, as well as not work, period. I would like to get this thing firmed up.*

B: *What I'm going to do this afternoon in fact, I am going to dictate me a memo to lay this whole thing out. I feel like Estes must have a contact with some other lawyer. I'll work me a memo up, since at this stage I feel like I should not call the shots for him. I'll just give the facts I know and let someone else make a decision for him, because I'm prejudiced, I think he ought to do it.*

R: *Yeah.*

B: *O.K.?*

R: *When do you think I can get back with you so I can pull off the manpower situation?*

B: *I will try this afternoon to visit with whoever is going to represent Estes and I think we ought to be in a position to give some kind of answer. . . let's see, tomorrow is Friday. I'll try like hell to give you something to-*

morrow. . . That's as fast as I can work.

R: *Because I will like to end. . . We're talking about not wanting any publicity. . . nobody's looking for publicity that I know of. . . As soon as you let me know, I'll set up a time with Judge Mahon, get the information brought up. . . he's supposed to be over there at 2:00 on Monday and Tuesday afternoons.*

B: *Right. We are firm on removing Sue out of that first fraud indictment.*

R: *Well, I think, I'm going to go ahead and say yes. I'm going to. Copenhaver seems to be important to necessitate it. I would like to have her testimony, because I don't think Estes would like to see Copenhaver walk away from this thing. . . he's been a big part.*

B: *I know it. One thing about it, if somebody is not threatened by any prosecutions, it is awful hard to justify it.*

R: *That's right. It will probably be easier just to set it up. I don't think really we need a lot. We've got enough circumstantial evidence and documentary evidence. If we just have a warm body to say exactly what happened, I don't think they will be in a position to fight it. So, the answer to that would be, in return for her testimony, that we will grant her immunity.*

B: *O.K., and working it this way on the information, would keep Pam and John L. and I completely out of it.*

R: *Uh Huh. It would be that Billie Sol Estes and uh Raymond Horton and others. . . in the event that Horton went to trial we would have to have a Bill of*

Particulars on it.

B: A Bill of Particulars. Right. Now we'll get back together tomorrow. . . .

IN HIS BRIEF, IRWIN SUMMARIZED the negotiating process and quoted Daddy as saying that Bryant "offered me the amount of $1,200 per month if I would accept the Justice Department's plea bargain."

Irwin maintained that the threat of indictment of Daddy's family was used to coerce him into agreement. Daddy hadn't wanted to plea bargain because he felt he was innocent, and he wanted to fight it out.

Back in the 60's, Daddy could have plea-bargained, and, instead of the 15-year sentence he got, he could have gotten a five-year sentence and been out of jail in six months, but he felt then he was innocent and wanted to go to trial. This time, we did not want to go through another trial. I wasn't so much afraid of being indicted myself because I didn't think they could convict me. But after another family conference, Daddy decided that it would be easier on all of us, himself included, just to plea bargain, go to jail for a little while and get them off our backs.

At a rare press conference, Daddy told the press that he was considering the government's offer because he could not "put my loved ones through that." Uncle John L. said the family would not allow Daddy to accept the offer. We were innocent of concealing assets and would gladly go to trial. I was in Dallas at the time with my daughter Tricia for major surgery on her hip. Uncle John L. called and said, "Pam, I don't want you to get upset, but I have heard that they are going to arrest you today. . . and me." He continued, "Don't worry, just go with them, and I will come and get you out." So I spent that day nursing Tricia, wondering what to wear for an arrest and how on earth Uncle John L. could get me out if he were arrested too.

When it began to look like the U.S. Attorney was serious about arresting the entire family, Daddy accepted the plea bargain offer, but the agreement depended on the cooperation of the parole board. If Daddy were to plead guilty as specified, he would be automatically in violation of his parole, therefore the parole board had to be party to the agreement.

The parole board refused and threatened to revoke Daddy's parole, and so it was decided, once again, to go to trial.

THE GOVERNMENT WAS SET TO BRING three separate charges against Daddy. One was for fraud in inducing Jap Burkett to invest $50,000 in Permian Petroleum and Billy Pyron's Frenchman's Creek CB business. Another was for selling non-existent steam cleaners for oil field equipment to leasing companies. That sounded very much like the deals for fertilizer tanks in the 60s. The last was for conspiracy to conceal assets from the IRS. That was the indictment that his family and friends were tied to. At the time we decided to go to trial, we had no idea whether the government would follow through on its threat to indict all of us or whether it would drop charges against everyone except Daddy.

The IRS successfully sued Daddy and Mother in 1976 for about $24 million in unpaid taxes, interest and penalties due for the rich years of 1959 to 1962. Daddy's attorneys responded to the suit by saying that "the IRS, after 14 years of surveillance, audits, and investigation, well knows the defendant has no property which is subject to any tax lien now in existence."

What happened to the $20-odd million Daddy is supposed to have made in his big swindle of finance companies in the 1960s has remained a mystery. But Daddy says, "There is no mystery to Billie Sol Estes. The solution to the mystery is that there is no hidden money. Money means nothing to me. It never has. As long as I have friends, that's the only important thing."

After word got out of possible indictments of family members and friends, Daddy held a press conference. He told the press, "They've got my attorney, Jack Bryant, put in a position where he can avoid indictment if he'll get me to plead guilty." They have threatened to indict my daughter, Pam, my brother, John L., my former secretary, Sue Goolsby, and my attorney. I never thought anything could shake me, but when they got on my daughter they just went too far. And if it could happen to my daughter, it could happen to your daughter.

". . . And Dr. John, it would be like jumping on Jesus Christ to jump on Dr. John. Bring me one man that will bring and bear a bad word against that man. I have a beloved brother who has stood beside me all my years. He has supported me, sent every child I had to college. This is just wrong."

But Daddy said he still had a "deep faith in God, a deep faith in the American system of justice. I know justice will prevail. I just believe that in this country, if they're allowed to do this sort of thing that's just going too far."

Rolfe, when told about Daddy's press conference, said, "I'm restricted by the guidelines of the U.S. Justice Department and by the Privacy Act from commenting on any aspect of any pending criminal case. "In theory," Rolfe said, "we're not even supposed to comment on whether a criminal investigation is going on. But Estes, by going to the press to try his case in the press has waived his rights under the Privacy Act. Estes has got his cake and is eating it too."

The next few months in the spring and summer of 1979 were spent traveling back and forth between Abilene and Dallas to pre-trial hearings, conferences, and grand jury investigations. I was summoned before the federal grand jury in Dallas and told to bring business records. The grand jury claimed to be trying to determine whether or not Daddy was funneling money for me to hold for him. We had precious little money at that time and their attempts to prove that what little we had were Daddy's "hidden assets" would have been pathetic and laughable except for the fact that we were having to go deep into debt to defend ourselves.

Throughtout all this persecution, I tried to keep some sense of humor. Once I was summoned to the federal building in Abilene to make a deposition. I wore a sweater with writing across the front that said, "Nobody's Perfect." Jack Bryant, who met me outside the building was furious. "I would send you home to change," he said, "but there isn't time."

During Daddy's first trial I experienced all the bewildering emotion of a child watching a parent under attack and I thought I left behind the depths of that wrenching experience but I was wrong. As an adult I would have the added responsibility of trying to keep all our lives together, worry about money to keep us fed and sheltered as well as the anxiety of the trial itself.

So I began to prepare myself for what I supposed was going to be two weeks of sheer hell. I was wrong again. It was going to be six weeks.

XIII CHAPTER

"I Got My Tit in a Wringer"

During the four weeks we spent at the Dallas trial, we stayed at the old Adolphus Hotel. At that time the Adolphus lobby had been remodeled, but the rooms upstairs were still archaic. We had two rooms which had the dividing wall knocked out to form one big room with two baths. The hotel shower wasn't big enough for me or Daddy to fit into, and the sink was so small that when you brushed your teeth you had to stick your head under the faucet to gargle.

Our attorney, Jerry Irwin, had a room above ours on another floor, and Ray Horton had a room of his own. Our family of five adults, children, spouses, grandchildren and different visiting relatives spent six weeks in this one room. It was wall-to-wall rollaway beds. Mother and Daddy had a double rollaway bed and the rest were single beds.

The hotel didn't like us because of the number of towels we used and because there was no way the maids could clean properly with everyone's possessions scattered around.

Members from one of the Churches of Christ brought us food packages full of spam, potted meat and tuna fish. With that and our crock pot we managed to survive.

One of the biggest problems with that number of people in such a small space is sanitation and personal hygiene. We all tried to keep our areas scrupulously clean so as not to offend each other. After we had been at the Adolphus for two weeks, confined in the room with all the people, tuna, spam, lack of towels, and lack of privacy, my sister, Dawn, almost hysterical, noticed Fred had athlete's foot. We had no medicine available, so Dawn, having had training in dental hygiene, did the best that she could. She took a can of disinfectant spray and sprayed his feet twice a day. His athlete's foot was soon cured, but for the rest of the trial, as inconvenient as it was, we only had one bathroom to use because Fred got one to himself.

We were sure that our room was tapped or bugged. We had already heard tapes of our conversations in court, so there was no reason to suppose they had stopped bugging us just because the trial had started. At night when we were all ready to go to sleep we had a good time, one of the rare light moments of our day, saying goodnight to each other and to our eavesdroppers.

Ray Horton paid for our room, and as I recall, Walter and I paid for many of Daddy's and Mother's meals. In fact, that was how we lost our American Express card. It was taken away because the month after the trial, we were unable to pay the bill in one installment. They sent us a letter and said to cut it in two, put it in an envelope, and mail it to them, so Walter cut it in two, put it in an envelope, and wrote them and told them where they could stick it.

Ray and his family were very kind to us during the trial and never expressed any hostility or resentment to us or to Daddy. Ray would not have gotten into any trouble except that he was associated with Daddy. His trial was the result of fallout from that association. He was a very successful man before he met Daddy, and his association was intended to help Daddy more than enrich himself. Mrs. Horton, who was a very religious person, told us that she was praying for us every day. Uncle John L. was to later say, "He was the only friend your Daddy ever had."

JERRY IRWIN WANTED TO ENLIST the aid of Racehorse Haynes in jury selection. Jerry said, "If Racehorse selects the jury, the case is half won." When we told Jerry we couldn't afford Racehorse, Jerry replied, "I'll sell some of my own personal property, if I have to, so we can pay him."

Unfortunately, Cullen Davis' trial ran at the same time as Daddy's, and Racehorse was busy with that so he wasn't available to help with Daddy's defense even if we could have paid him. Jerry had complete confidence and admiration for Racehorse's ability. "He could get the truth out of a dead man," he said.

Despite our admiration for Racehorse and our desire to hire him to defend Daddy, we were certain that Jerry was on his way to being the best defense attorney in the state.

At the jury selection, each prospective juror was asked if he had ever heard of Billie Sol Estes. At first we found the many wild answers funny. In fact, Irwin told us at one point that if we didn't stop laughing we would have to leave the room. We quickly sobered up and realized that the many misperceptions about Daddy were serious and weren't going to help his case. Some of the jurors thought he was an embezzler. Some thought he had non-existent grain elevators. I think one or two thought he was a murderer or rapist.

There were a number of people who really wanted to be on the jury. They would be asked if they had ever heard of Billie Sol Estes, and they would look both ways and quickly say, "No." One elderly taxi driver when asked what he knew of Daddy, said, "All I know is he's the finest man who ever lived." He was excused instantly.

The prosecution didn't want any women on the jury because women tend to have a natural sympathy for Daddy. Irwin didn't care whether the jurors were men or women. He wanted the more intelligent jurors because he felt they would more likely understand the evidence—or lack of it.

Judge Hill, himself, questioned a number of the prospective jurors. He read a list of prospective witnesses and asked if anyone knew any of them. It turned out that one man had been involved in a lawsuit with Billy Pyron, and so he was excused.

Among the witnesses the government listed was Copenhaver, who had already plea bargained and been sent to jail for his role in the steam cleaner deal. The ironic thing is that if he had pled not guilty he would have been acquitted along with Daddy and Ray Horton on that count. With the selection of an attractive middle-aged blonde woman who kept looking adoringly at Judge Hill, the jury was completed and the prosecution was ready to present its case.

Part of the evidence presented by Jim Rolfe was a judgement showing that Mother and Daddy together owed the government about $52 million in back income taxes, penalties and interest. One of the most alarming things about that IRS claim, which has been kicking around since 1962, is every time it is mentioned it has grown by several million dollars. Because of the compounding of interest and penalties, it grows daily and will eventually rise to an amount sufficient to wipe out the government's budget deficits.

OUR OLD FRIEND, WALT PERRY, ALIAS Walt Placko, testified that while he was working undercover, posing as a Chicago businessman, he made a deal with Daddy for $3 million. Under cross examination he admitted that no deal was ever signed, but he said, "I never intended to sign anything."

He was then asked if someone had blown his cover, and he admitted that they had when Daddy called the number he had given him and someone answered "Internal Revenue Service."

All of this was supposed to prove that Daddy was concealing assets. Even Uncle John L. was called by the government because they believed that he was also a party to a conspiracy. Among other things Uncle John L. testified that he had given us about $95,000 since 1962 for living expenses. He said much of Daddy's problems stemmed from the impossible parole conditions. He said all Daddy's big talk about big deals was mostly bragging and had no substance. "It's like an incurable disease," he testified.

Jap Burkett was probably the most damaging witness against Daddy. He told how he had been persuaded by Daddy to invest $50,000 in Billy Pyron's CB business, which later failed. He appeared to be just a simple old farmer who had suffered during imprisonment in World War II, where he got the nickname, "Jap," and now he was suffering at the hands of a master swindler. The jury ate it up.

The charge on which Daddy and Ray were acquitted was very complex. According to government witnesses this is the way the operation was supposed to work. A company called Atomic Enterprises in San Antonio was to manufacture the steam cleaners. They were then bought by leasing companies on orders from Ray

Horton's oil company. When Horton's company defaulted on its lease payments to the leasing companies, the leasing companies tried to repossess them, only to discover that they could not be found. They had either been stolen or had never existed. Many people, remembering Daddy's earlier scandal involving non-existent fertilizer tanks, preferred to believe, not only had the steam cleaners never existed, but that Daddy must somehow be behind it all. The jury chose to believe otherwise.

One of the government's witnesses was Frank J. Fuell from Midland, who testified that in 1975 he passed along almost $34,000 to Daddy in cash. Fuell, like Copenhaver, pled guilty in a plea bargain for his part in the scheme. Ray testified that he tried to make good the loan payments on the cleaners when he discovered that Atomic Enterprises had not delivered or even manufactured them.

FRED MICHAELIS, WHO WAS AFFECTIONATELY called the "front" because the prosecution was convinced that was what he was. He was one of the star witnesses at the trial. Fred was almost like an idiot savant. He was brilliant in some areas, and in others almost retarded. He had to do all Daddy's driving because Daddy usually had his driver's license revoked for having too many tickets.

Fred and Daddy had single handedly done all the taping of witnesses with their makeshift electronic equipment. They also bugged some offices of potential government witnesses. They took a tape recorder and placed a bug under a table at the Chit Chat Club, a topless bar in Abilene that employed mostly Asian dancers. Fred would then invite people there, buy them drinks, and engage them in conversations in order to get a really honest version of information from the potential witness to be used in the trial.

Then Fred would make a copy of the recording, and when that particular person was subpoenaed, he would go see them and play the tape for them to refresh their memories. That way, the witness would know that when they testified for the government we would have the taped version which had been given, not under oath, but at the Chit Chat Club. After meetings, Fred would very crudely in his illegible handwriting and poor spelling, label the tapes, put them in shoe boxes, and then into a big suitcase, to be used in Daddy's defense against the government.

As the trial continued, the prosecution built up, as a major part of their case, the idea that Fred was the front for Billie Sol Estes; that he was the man who was actually doing the business for Daddy. So by the time Fred finally took the stand every juror was expecting a polished con artist. Not Fred. Fred had had some 50 careers in his lifetime. He had been a hairdresser, the owner of a wig shop, a pilot, a moonie, had sold flowers in Austin and was an extra in a horror movie.

When Fred finally took the stand he caused Judge Hill to nearly go into cardiac arrest. Fred was unable to answer a question directly. He was asked where he lived. He said he lived at 70 Castle Drive, Abilene, Texas (Mother and Daddy's address).

They asked him where he got transportation. He said that there was a Cadillac parked in the driveway with keys in it. They asked him where he got the gas. He said if there was gas in it he drove it, if there wasn't he didn't. They asked him how he ate. He said he ate whatever was left over. They asked him about his previous work record. He said, "Well, I don't know your Honor, do you want to know before I was Moonie or after I was a Moonie?"

Judge Hill said, "We don't want to hear about you being a Moonie."

Fred said, "Well, the reason I got kicked out of the Moonies, Your Honor, was because they said I asked too many questions."

Judge Hill was thoroughly exasperated by Fred Michaelis' testimony because it was destroying the government's credibility. The jury could clearly see that Fred was incapable of being a front for anyone.

During the trial, Irwin got an inside tip that the Feds were going to confiscate Daddy's Rolex watch while he was in court. So Daddy immediately borrowed a Timex, and when they came over to him and told him to hold out his arm, they were furious to see a Timex instead of the expensive Rolex, which had been a gift from Daddy's employees in the 50s.

THE DEFENSE PRESENTATION WAS VERY brief. It lasted only six hours in contrast to the two weeks used by the prosecution. Ray's defense also took about one day. The most wrenching part of the trial for Daddy was when my sister took the stand and testified about how she had worked since she was a teenager to help the family. Daddy broke into tears at that point, and the judge sent the jury out of the room, and we all gathered around Daddy and cried with him.

Daddy also testified in his own defense and tried to convince the court that he had no hidden assets. He admitted under cross-examination that since he had spent six and a half years in prison, "Regretfully, I have become a liar." Mother says that Daddy just likes to brag and people shouldn't take everything he says seriously. "If someone tells a big one," she says, "Sol has to match it." Daddy couldn't stand being poor. It was a great blow to his ego to not be in charge of his life and to not be able to wheel and deal as he had in the

60s. Bragging was one way he made up for it.

Jerry Irwin's defense argument was based on the fact that the prosecution, after spending over a million dollars on an investigation and trial, had not introduced any proof that Daddy had any assets to conceal. We felt that Jerry Irwin, with almost no resources to prepare a defense, did a brilliant job.

When the verdict was announced and Daddy was once again pronounced "guilty," we were all shocked. Mother collapsed. Fred, who was standing next to her and Daddy, picked her up, and with the aid of my brother-in-law, Danny, and my husband, Walter, they carried her down the street all the way back to the hotel. This picture of Fred carrying Mother will remain with me always and will forever endear him to me.

The U.S. Attorney's assistant prosecutors and IRS men had assembled for the verdict. When it was read, they all cheered. As we left the court, crying again, one of the young lawyers looked at me and said, "We finally got him."

SENTENCING WAS SET FOR AUGUST 7, 1979, almost a month later. In the meantime, a number of jurors asked for lenience for Daddy. Many of them cried and apologized to us, but they felt they had to convict him. One of the jurors by the name of Ray Loggins testified that he had been ill and had been forced into his decision.

The jury foreman Earnest Cotton said, "The trial itself was punishment enough."

Nevertheless, on August 7, Judge Hill sentenced Daddy to 10 years in jail and Ray Horton to five. Daddy was convicted on two counts and acquitted of the steam cleaner charge. His sentence was two consecutive 5-year terms. Ray was acquitted also of the steam cleaner charge but convicted of conspiracy to conceal assets and was sentenced to one 5-year term. Both were sent to La Tuna, near El Paso, where they were roommates briefly until Ray was released after serving just a few months.

After the sentencing, Uncle John L. responded the next day with a statement to the press that said in part, "To convict Billie Sol of intent to avoid income taxes without proving the existence of the income is. . . unjustifiable. To convict any person of attempt to defraud the government of income without proving in fact that income was actually received makes a mockery of justice."

ON AUGUST 12, 1979, DADDY LEFT FOR Dallas again. Every time he went to Dallas we were afraid he wouldn't be allowed to come back, so each time we had a going away dinner. This time only Mother and Fred would accompany him. He was going to a hearing for a motion for a new trial. Sue Goolsby's trial was due to begin the following day.

Sue was very upset and had dreaded this day for months. The U.S. Attorney called her repeatedly, attempting to get her to plead guilty to one count of conspiracy. They promised that if she pled guilty, they would guarantee her a probated or suspended sentence and give her a new identity and set her up in the location of her choice.

Her lawyer, Dru Nevill of Oklahoma City, thought that she had a very good chance of winning, but then Daddy's attorney had expressed the same opinion about his case.

Daddy's hearing was scheduled for 1 p.m. that same day. Irwin had filed a motion for mistrial.

We were relieved when Daddy called to tell us that the charges against Sue had been dropped for insufficient evidence and because of an affidavit from Jap Burkett stating that he felt that she did not try to defraud him.

The motion for mistrial lasted one hour and 15 minutes. Judge Hill ruled that Daddy's trial was valid despite juror Ray Loggins' testimony that he had been influenced by reading and hearing news reports during the trial.

However, when Judge Hill questioned him, he admitted that he agreed with the newspaper's account, so Judge Hill said that he did not believe that the news accounts had been prejudicial.

Judge Hill overruled the motion and Daddy was immediately taken into custody on a parole revocation warrant. He was placed in Dallas County Jail and was to be sent back to La Tuna Prison at El Paso.

The issuance of the warrant had been kept secret until a week before when the Parole Commission notified U.S. Marshal Peoples. Peoples said he was instructed to tell no one of the warrant.

When Daddy told Mother what was happening, she was even more shocked than he. When Mother called to tell me of Daddy's arrest, my sister, Sue and Walter were with me in the office. We cried, then we called the rest of the family.

Then we called Daddy's mother. I said, "MaMa, they've arrested Daddy. We just wanted to tell you before you heard it on the news." "Thank you," she said, "I won't watch the news."

We called Mother's parents and learned that grandmother had apparently suffered a heart attack. Fortunately, it later turned out to be just an irregular heart beat, and she came home within a few days. However, we didn't know that at the time, so we asked Fred to drive Mother to Brady, Texas to see Grandmother.

We didn't tell Mother about Grandmother's emergency hospitalization because we didn't know how well she could handle more bad news after the shock of Daddy's arrest. We told Fred we didn't want Mother to know about her mother's hospitilization until she got to Brady, and he took us literally. When they reached the city limits, Fred said, "Pat, where is the hospital? Your mother is dying. She had a heart attack."

THE PICTURES OF DADDY HANDCUFFED and in the little cage in Dallas will remain the saddest memory of my life. Looking at them now, all the low points of my life come rushing back, and they still have the power to send me into a depression. On the other hand, when I ask myself, would I have traded my father for one who worked at the hardware store from 9 to 5 and who kept our lives always on a constant keel, I have to answer that I would not.

Despite everything—the extreme lows of our lives—life with Daddy has been an intoxicating roller-coaster ride. I treasure the memories of growing up as Daddy's darling little girl, in and out of limousines and planes, huge parties and political rallies and shopping sprees to Neiman's in Dallas—and an occasional cozy family gathering.

Daddy used to say, "The sweetest fruit is fartherest out on the limb. I like to walk out as far as I can on that limb. If the limb breaks, I know how far I can go next time." When Daddy comes home again, it will be "next time."

EPILOGUE

On December 21, 1982, our whole family was feeling depressed because we had just learned that Daddy had been turned down for an early release from prison. I was working at my desk when I received one of the saddest calls I can remember, and there have been many. A friend called and said, "Did you hear that Jerry Irwin was killed?" My first thought was that he had been murdered for trying to help Daddy. My second thought was disbelief. Our "Little Peacock" was too full of life to be dead. He had such a full life ahead, I thought.

Immediately, I called his office in Longview and a tearful secretary said, "I'm sorry. It's true. We can't believe it either." Jerry had been killed in a boating accident.

Throughout the last 20 years many people who have been connected with Daddy's case are now dead. Henry Marshall, the Agriculture Department official in charge of cotton allotments in Texas in the early 60's was the first; and the cause of his death is still a mystery. Since then, Harold Orr, the President of Superior Manufacturing, who pleaded guilty to mail fraud in the fertilizer tank deal, killed himself before entering prison. Likewise, George Krutilek, the accountant who helped all the farmers in that same deal to falsify their financial statements, also committed suicide.

John Cofer, Daddy's first defense attorney, is dead as is the judge at the El Paso trial, Judge Thomason. Uncle Bob died of cancer in 1966.

Dr. John Dunn, the man who started it all with stories in his Pecos newspaper, was recently quoted in Jane Sumner's column in *Dallas Life Magazine* as saying, "Estes is not the most guilty party. I'd be glad to go before a parole board on his behalf. He has served more time than a murderer."

If there is anything positive to be said about a prison experience it is that at a white-collar federal prison you're apt to meet some of the most interesting people in the country. Daddy has met many such men. They have been captains of industry, brilliant entrepreneurs, soldiers of fortunes or just plain risk-taking adventurers.

One of the men he roomed with at Big Spring Prison camp was a doctor from Austin who was a friend of Willie Nelson. Dr. Young, who was allowed to work out in the community, volunteered to recruit Willie Nelson to perform at a benefit concert.

As a result of Daddy's work promoting the concert from inside the prison, he contrived to introduce his family to Willie. Daddy and Willie became friends and still correspond.

My husband said, when he heard we were going to meet Willie Nelson at the prison, "This is just another thing Sol has dreamed up that will never come off," but nevertheless we all were there at the appointed time, and we met Willie. He was very nice to us and told us that any time we came to one of his concerts, we could have backstage passes. I introduced him to my daughters, and he said to my youngest, Amy, "I have a daughter named Amy about your age. Would you like to have my bandana?" He untied the bandana around his head and offered it to her. Amy replied, "Ugh. Gross. No." Later when I got her ouside and asked her why she was so rude, she said, "Oh, Mother, it was so sweaty." We went to a Willie Nelson concert in San Angelo, and he invited us to sit on the edge of the stage with his friends during the concert.

On July 21, 1983, Daddy filed suit against the Bureau of Prisons and U.S. Parole Commission for $52 million, alleging a violation of his civil, constitutional and human rights.

When Daddy entered prison, a tentative parole date of December 15, 1982 had been projected. After review by the National Parole Commission, the parole date had been rescheduled for December 15, 1983. Daddy successfully contested the severity category for his offense but was unable to get a re-evaluation of his guidelines. (Severity category and guidelines are bureaucratic clap-trap by which the prison keeps track of a prisoner's status.)

When Ray Horton's sentence was reduced, Judge Hill also resentenced Daddy in order to allow the Parole Commission to grant him parole at its discretion. However, they left his parole date unchanged.

Daddy's suit claims that the prison board's failure to abide by the standard practices of basing parole on strict guidelines is arbitrary and violates his civil rights.

GETTING OUT OF PRISON WON'T SOLVE all Daddy's problems, but in many ways, will only exacerbate them. If his parole guidelines are anything like those of 1971 he will be effectively prohibited from working. The 1971 guidelines forbade him to be self-employed or to work in promotional activities. That forced him eventually to work sub rosa since "promotional activity" is the only line of work Daddy knows. Why else would any employer want him. Also, the vagueness of the guidelines gave the parole officer enormous arbitrary power over Daddy since anything that advances or enhances a business could be called promotional activity.

It is a rare employer who would hire Daddy. As soon as he goes to work for a company, that company is immediately put under surveillance. Its telephones are tapped, and all the company activities come under close scrutiny by various government agencies.

Since Daddy has a $52 million judgment against him from the IRS, he is not allowed to own anything, He is not even allowed to maintain a personal checking account because, if he were to deposit money in the bank, it would be immediately seized by the IRS. Since he is not allowed to go into business, the prospect of paying off the $52 million judgment is ludicrously slim. Interest is accumulating on the judgment at the rate of about $3 million a year, and the prospect of paying it off during his lifetime, working for someone else, would mean he would have to hold down the presidencies of General Motors and Standard Oil simultaneously and live on bread and water just to keep abreast of the interest payments. It's like the Red Queen in *Through the Looking Glass* who tells Alice, who is losing ground while running at top speed, "You have to run as fast as you can to stay in the same place. If you want to get anywhere, you must run much faster than that." In effect, Daddy has been given a life sentence by the IRS.

Nevertheless, on November 15, 1983, Daddy is scheduled to be placed in the federal half-way house in Abilene which is run by the Salvation Army. Coming as it does just at the Christmas rush, Daddy will be just in time to put on a Santa Claus suit and ring the bell for the Salvation Army out at the Abilene Mall—with someone else holding the pot to collect the money, of course.

WALTER, MY EX-HUSBAND, WHO STOOD BY ME during some of the most difficult times in my life is no longer standing by me. In late 1981 and early 1982 Walter's behavior began to subtly change. He had recently made a job change and had increased his drinking. He became moody and sullen, and it seemed to be harder for us to communicate. I thought he was just having trouble with his diabetes. I was wrong. As it turned out, he was having trouble with his manicurist.

It was I who first suggested that he have his hands manicured. Walter frequently went hunting, played golf, and dug in the garden so his hands were always rough with broken nails. I thought a manicure would make him feel good.

One day in February in 1982 we sat down on the couch in the den to have a talk. Walter said to me, "I've been wanting to tell you that I think I should move into an apartment."

I was shocked. "What did you say?" I replied. After all, we had a lovely home. "I'm just not happy," he said. Walter had always had such a consistently even mood that I had never suspected that anything could be wrong. I, who have such a wide range of emotional expression, never leave any doubt when I am happy or depressed, but Walter was different.

I was so shocked and upset that I called Walter's parents in Wichita Falls and told them that I thought Walter was having a nervous breakdown. They rushed to Abilene immediately and were here in less than three hours.

They sat down with Walter and had a long talk and tried to understand what was wrong—still no hint of the manicurist. We all decided that Walter's diabetes was out of control so it was decided that he should have a complete physical.

I went with him to the doctor's office and watched him fill out the doctor's questionaire. I was puzzled when under the question "How is your sex life" Walter put "wonderful." I thought I knew for a fact that Walter's sex life had been inactive for over a year.

A more modern wife would have become suspicious when Walter started going golfing and forgetting to take his clubs or would return from an afternoon quail hunting freshly showered.

It's at about this time that a friend always decides that it's time for the wife to know where her husband is spending his time—and a lot of his money. This friend, who was a man who worked for me, took me over to the local Motel 6 and showed me Walter's truck. I had to finally face the fact that Walter must be in one of those rooms, although I did not yet know with whom. I went to the office and tried to call him on the phone and discovered that Motel 6's don't have phones. So I asked the desk clerk which room he was in. He wouldn't tell me so I went back outside and honked my horn in front of the motel. The clerk told me if I didn't leave he was going to call the police, which he did. I had a key to Walter's truck, so I asked my friend to drive it home, and I settled in to wait.

The police came and told me that I would have to stop honking. I decided to wait him out. I knew that he would soon have to have a meal to prevent insulin shock, and it would not be long before he would come out. After a while, I saw a hand emerge from around the door of one of the rooms. On its wrist was the gold Rolex diamond-dial watch I had given Walter for our anniversary, and further up the arm, I recognized the sleeve of a shirt I had given him.

When he and the manicurist finally came out, I recognized her as someone who had sat next to us in church every Sunday. She had been very friendly and helpful to me. She had even taken our children bowling and on other outings. I also had noticed that she never took communion in church.

Since she didn't have a ride home I told them both to get into the car. "Now I know," I said to her, "why you don't ever take communion in church."

Walter and I had a long talk and decided to try to work out the problems in our marriage, but Walter was too much in love. He and the manicurist ran away together.

A few weeks later, on April Fool's Day, I was looking through the paper for a dollar movie to take the kids to and the name Tedford caught my eye. Walter had filed for divorce, and it was no April Fool's joke. Later, the manicurist ran off and left him, and he married a successful woman he had known since childhood.

By June 1, the stress was too much for me, and I became the first patient in the new stress center, which was just opening at Hendrick Medical Center in Abilene.

I spent seven weeks there. When I came out I had a new resolve to turn my life around, and I settled down to my real estate business, my children and my book, and I have not looked back.

ON NOVEMBER 15, 1983, DADDY EMERGED from prison once more, the TV lights glaring in the early morning darkness, his inmate friends shouting goodbys and waving placards. He is all set to embark on a new creer, remembering and writing down his memoirs. Now that he has decided to break the 20 year silence, he is determined to speak to whomever will listen and talk about how the world of government contracts really works.

I have a feeling that he will be telephoning me every morning at 5 a.m. to get me started on my day. I hope he can now use all that energy and ability in a positive way to make some real difference in the world—much as he has done for me in encouraging me to keep going. Like him, I don't want to look back, but forward. There are many things I want to accomplish. This is just the beginning.

APPENDIX

IN THE UNITED STATES DISTRICT COURT

FOR THE NORTHERN DISTRICT OF TEXAS

DALLAS DIVISION

UNITED STATES OF AMERICA *
*
V. * CRIMINAL NO. ______________
* (18 U.S.C. 371)
BILLIE SOL ESTES *

PLEA AGREEMENT

The following plea agreement has been made pursuant to the Court's approval:

1. Billie Sol Estes will enter a plea to a one-count information, a copy of which is attached hereto, charging him with a violation of Title 18 U.S.C., Section 371, Section 1341, and Section 2314, which count carries a fine of not more than $10,000 or imprisonment of not more than five years, or both. If such plea is withdrawn for any reason or reasons other than those enumerated in the paragraphs below then this plea agreement is null and void.

2. The United States Attorney will not present any further charges, either by the filing of any further informations or the presentation of any proposed indictments with reference to the following "transactions":

A. That series of occurrences whereby certain leasing companies allegedly purchased approximately thirty-six chemical cleaners from a company known as Atomic Enterprises of San Antonio, Texas.

B. That series of occurrences whereby certain individuals and companies had various business transactions with an entity known as Mfg. Rep. of Frenchman's Creek, and its various divisions and subsidiaries.

C. Any charges relating to violations of Title 26 U.S.C., Section 7206(1) involving unreported income of approximately $33,000 for the year 1975.

PLEA AGREEMENT - Page 1

1. Plea bargain agreement. *The parole commission threw a monkey wrench into this agreement because, if Daddy accepted it, it automatically meant he acknowledged parole violation.*

D. Any occurrences concerning Permian Chicago, Inc., Solex Realty, Vandelia Properties, Inc., and Davida, Inc.

E. Any occurrences concerning the alleged R. K. Horton - John L. Estes Trust.

3. It is further part of this "plea bargain" that the United States Attorney's Office for the Northern District of Texas will recommend to the United States Parole Commission that Billie Sol Estes' parole be revoked for technical violations of the terms of his parole for a period commencing with the beginning date of any sentence imposed hereunder and ending no later than the date of the expiration of his present parole, and will further recommend that the parole not be revoked for a period of time commencing with the date that Billie Sol Estes was released from the Federal Corrections Institution; and that Billie Sol Estes be sentenced after the United States Parole Commission has acted on this recommendation; and that the United States Attorney nor any of his agents or representatives, shall hereafter intercede to impose objection to the release on parole of defendant Billie Sol Estes on any sentence imposed hereunder.

4. That the plea of guilty entered pursuant to this "plea bargain" agreement shall be conditioned upon the acceptance by the U.S. Parole Commission of that recommendation made by the U.S. Attorney in Paragraph 3 above and failure on the part of the U.S. Parole Commission to accept, and act on, at any time, that recommendation of the U.S. Attorney's Office in Paragraph 3 above shall make null and void this "plea bargain" agreement and the defendant shall have the right to withdraw his plea of guilty made pursuant thereto.

5. That Billie Sol Estes agrees that he will enter a plea as set forth above for the reason that he is guilty of the offense charged in the information attached hereto, and for no

other reason; and that no promises or agreements have been made by the U.S. Attorney other than those enumerated herein.

6. That John L. Estes, Patsy Estes, Pamela Tedford, Walter Tedford and Ms. Sue Goolsby will not be prosecuted by the United States Attorney's Office for the Northern District of Texas for any of the matters enumerated or referred to herein or within any attachment.

BILLIE SOL ESTES
Defendant

KENNETH J. MIGHELL
United States Attorney

BY

G. BROCKETT IRWIN
Attorney for Defendant

JIM ROLFE
Assistant United States Attorney

IN THE UNITED STATES DISTRICT COURT

FOR THE NORTHERN DISTRICT OF TEXAS

DALLAS DIVISION

UNITED STATES OF AMERICA *
*
V. * CRIMINAL NO.______
* (18 U.S.C. 371)
BILLIE SOL ESTES *

Stipulation of Evidence:

It is agreed and stipulated by and between the defendant Billie Sol Estes, Mr. G. Brockett Irwin (attorney for the defendant) and the United States Attorneys Office for the Northern District of Texas that the following facts would and could be elicited from witnesses and exhibits:

1. In the year 1971 the defendant, Billie Sol Estes, owed the United States of America in excess of $10,000,000 in income taxes, penalties, and interest for the years 1959, 1961, and 1962.

2. Beginning in the year 1971 and continuing until August 5, 1977, Billie Sol Estes entered into several business transactions with other persons who would hold or control in their name or names, and in the names of other persons and entities certain assets of value, and portions and percentages of business transactions which belonged to Billie Sol Estes or were due him, thereby concealing from the United States of America the ownership of Billie Sol Estes in those assets and portions and percentages of business transactions.

3. During the period January 1971 to July 1971, Raymond K. Horton and others made payments and effected various transfers of money, goods, and services for an on behalf of Billie Sol Estes.

4. During the period July 1971 to November 1971, Raymond K. Horton, Billie Sol Estes, and Buster Lea agreed that Raymond K. Horton would hold or control in his name the percentage or portion of business transactions entered into that belonged to defendant Billie Sol Estes.

STIPULATION OF EVIDENCE - Page 1

2. Stipulation of Evidence. If the plea-bargain agreement had been consummated, this would have been the summation of the evidence in the case.

5. On or about October 26, 1971, to evidence the above mentioned agreement, Raymond K. Horton and Buster Lea entered into a written agreement whereby the two-thirds ownership of certain business transactions would be held or controlled in the name of Raymond K. Horton.

6. During the period November 1971 to August 1973, Raymond K. Horton, Billie Sol Estes, and Buster Lea entered into certain business transactions whereby the below listed assets were purchased:

1. Nelson Estes' Property
2. Wheat Cattle Company
3. La Posada No. 2
4. Riverside Club
5. Slator Ranch
6. Kingston House Apartments
7. Vagabond Motel

7. During the period November 1971 to August 1973, Raymond K. Horton and Billie Sol Estes caused Billie Sol Estes' ownership, portion and percentage of the above mentioned entities to be held or controlled in the name of Raymond K. Horton.

8. On or about May 1, 1972, Raymond K. Horton, and BILLIE SOL ESTES caused Permian Petroleum Company, Inc., to place BILLIE SOL ESTES on the payroll of said corporation in the capacity of a dispatcher for said corporation's propane gas business.

9. On or about May 1, 1974, the exact date unknown, Raymond K. Horton caused to be transferred to his name, the stock of Growth Canadian, Inc., a Delaware corporation.

10. On or about May 21, 1974, the net assets of Permian Petroleum Company, Inc., were transferred to Growth Canadian, Inc.

11. On or about August 31, 1974, the Vagabond Motel was transferred to Growth Canadian, Inc.

12. During the period from January 1, 1974, to October 1, 1975, the exact dates being unknown to BILLIE SOL ESTES met and had conversations with Ray Barrett, both in person and over the telephone concerning financing of cleaner units through lease banks and financial companies. BILLIE SOL ESTES directed Ray

Barrett to contact lease companies for financing of high pressure chemical cleaners and also directed Ray Barrett to furnish financial statements of Raymond K. Horton to these companies.

13. On or about May 1, 1975, the exact date being unknown, Raymond K. Horton caused Growth Canadian, Inc., to change its name to Growth Energy, Inc.

14. On or about August 3, 1977, Raymond K. Horton, during a conversation with undercover special agents of the Internal Revenue Service, made statements concerning BILLIE SOL ESTES' interest in assets held by Raymond K. Horton.

15. On or about August 4, 1977, BILLIE SOL ESTES, during a conversation with undercover special agents of the Internal Revenue Service made statements concerning his interest in assets held by Raymond K. Horton.

16. On or about August 4, 1977, BILLIE SOL ESTES, during a telephone conversation with his attorney, Jack Bryant, made statements concerning his agreement with Raymond K. Horton.

In violation of Title 18, United States Code, Section 371.

BILLIE SOL ESTES
Defendant

KENNETH J. MIGHELL
United States Attorney

G. BROCKETT IRWIN
Counsel for Defendant

JAMES A. ROLFE
Assistant United States Attorney
1100 Commerce, Room 16G28
Dallas, Texas 75242
(214) 749-3491

COPY

IN THE UNITED STATES DISTRICT COURT FOR THE

NORTHERN DISTRICT OF TEXAS

ABILENE DIVISION

U. S. DISTRICT COURT NORTHERN DISTRICT OF TEXAS
FILED
APR 7 1976
JOSEPH McELROY, JR., CLERK
BY ______ Deputy

UNITED STATES OF AMERICA, Plaintiff	)	CIVIL ACTION NO.
v.	)	
BILLIE SOL ESTES, Defendant	)	CA1 76 19

C O M P L A I N T

Comes now the plaintiff, United States of America, by its attorney, Michael P. Carnes, United States Attorney for the Northern District of Texas, and for its cause of action complains and alleges as follows:

1. This is a civil action instituted by the United States of America for the purpose of reducing to judgment the federal income tax liabilities assessed against the defendant-taxpayer, Billie Sol Estates, for the years 1959, 1960, 1961 and 1962.

2. This action has been authorized and requested by the Chief Counsel of the Internal Revenue Service, and is brought pursuant to the direction of the Attorney General of the United States, under the provisions of Section 7401 and 7403 of the Internal Revenue Code of 1954.

3. Jurisdiction of this action is conferred upon this Court by Sections 1340 and 1345 of Title 28, United States Code, and Section 7402(a) of the Internal Revenue Code of 1954, for the reason that this is a civil action arising under the Internal Revenue laws of the United States.

3. IRS Complaint. This is the suit in which the IRS asked the court to render a judgment against Daddy for $21,094,955.33 for unpaid taxes.

4. The defendant-taxpayer, Billie Sol Estes, resides at 70 Castle Drive, Abilene, Texas, and is within the jurisdiction of this Court.

5. The defendant-taxpayer, Billie Sol Estes, filed a petition for an arrangement under Chapter XI of the Bankruptcy Act on or about April 7, 1962, in the United States District Court for the Western District of Texas, Pecos Division.

6. The defendant-taxpayer, Billie Sol Estes, was adjudicated a bankrupt, in the proceeding described in paragraph 5 above, on or about July 13, 1962.

7. The bankruptcy proceeding referred to in paragraphs 5 and 6 above was closed by Final Order of the Bankruptcy Court on or about December 5, 1969.

8. The defendant-bankrupt, Billie Sol Estes, was denied a discharge in bankruptcy on or about January 30, 1970.

9. On the dates set forth below, a delegate of the Secretary of the Treasury of the United States of America made assessments against the defendant-taxpayer, Billie Sol Estes, for federal income taxes, penalties and interest in the amounts and for the periods set forth in the table:

Taxable Period	Date of Assessment, Notice and Demand	Amount of Assessment	Total Assessed Unpaid Balance
1959	October 17, 1963	$ 345,250.34(T) 72,616.08(I) 172,625.17(P)	$ 590,491.59
1960	October 17, 1963	5,176,533.31(T) 778,181.87(I) 2,588,266.66(P)	8,542,981.84

Taxable Period	Date of Assessment, Notice and Demand	Amount of Assessment	Total Assessed Unpaid Balance
1961	August 9, 1963	$6,668,848.41(T) 527,569.84(I) 3,334,421.21(P)	$10,530,839.46
1962	January 23, 1967	1,166.619.05(T) 264,023.39(I)	1,430,642.44
			$21,094,955.33*

T - Indicates tax assessed.
I - Indicates interest assessed.
P - Indicates fraud penalty assessed, Sec. 6653(b), Internal Revenue Code of 1954.
* - Plus accrued interest as provided by law.

10. Notices of the assessments described in paragraph 9 above were given, and demands for payment thereof were duly made upon the defendant-taxpayer, Billie Sol Estes, but said defendant-taxpayer has neglected and refused to pay over the said amounts assessed against him, and as a result there is presently due and owing from the said defendant-taxpayer, Billie Sol Estes, to the United States of America the total assessed unpaid balance of $21,094,955.33, plus interest as provided by law.

WHEREFORE, the plaintiff, United States of America prays as follows:

1. That this Court find that the defendant-taxpayer, Billie Sol Estes, is indebted to the United States of America for federal income taxes, penalties and interest as described in paragraph 9 above in the amount of $21,094,955.33, plus accrued interest as provided by law.

2. That the United States be granted its costs in this proceeding and such other and further relief as to this Court seems just and proper.

MICHAEL P. CARNES
United States Attorney

By:

Claude D. Brown
Assistant United States Attorney

INDEX

Typeset in Times Roman and Clarendon Bold
by Custom Typographics
Manufactured in the United States of America
by R R Donnelley & Sons Company